THE CANADIAN *Junior* GREEN GUIDE

Dreaming of Earth

Last night I lay, and in my dream
I heard the planet give a scream.

People, people, don't you see?
This acid rain will be the death of me.

People, people, don't you care?
There's holes at the poles in the ozone layer.

People, people, can't you tell?
The greenhouse heat could make a living hell . . . .

I woke up then, with a fearful cry:
We've got to make that dream a lie!

Dennis Lee

TERI DEGLER is the author of several books including *Scuttlebutt*, *Straight from the Horse's Mouth* and *Love, Limits, and Consequences: A Practical Approach to Kids and Discipline*. She has an M.A. in special education and has been active in the environmental movement for many years.

DENNIS LEE is the author of such popular works for children as *Alligator Pie*, *Garbage Delight*, and *The Ordinary Bath*. He also was a contributor to the television program *Fraggle Rock*.

JOHN ELKINGTON, JULIA HAILES, and DOUGLAS HILL wrote *The Young Green Consumer Guide*, published in Great Britain by Victor Gollancz Ltd.

POLLUTION PROBE was established in 1969 as an independent, non-profit, research-based charitable organization. Through memberships or donations, more than 50,000 Canadians are Pollution Probe Partners. Pollution Probe researcher/writers for *The Canadian Junior Green Guide* are WILLIAM M. GLENN, an award-winning science writer and environmental consultant specializing in toxic chemical and hazardous waste issues, and RANDEE L. HOLMES, a freelance writer and researcher who contributed to *The Canadian Green Consumer Guide*, *The Canadian Green Calendar 1991*, and *Profit from Pollution Prevention*.

Acknowledgements

This book is the result of an exceptionally successful team effort, most notably between Teri Degler and Pollution Probe's representatives, William Glenn and Randee Holmes. Their tireless efforts and knowledgeable contributions made this project most worthwhile.

Teri Degler, William Glenn, and Randee Holmes, in turn, would like to thank Dennis Lee for his wonderful poetry contributions to the book. Thanks, too, are due Douglas Gibson, James Adams, and Lynn Flatley of McClelland & Stewart. Allen Tracey, Steve Van Rooy, and Michelle Clement of The Watt Group ensured the book's distinctive look and attractive presentation while the book's editor, Shaun Oakey, continually provided expertise, sound judgement, and patience.

Joey Moore and Janice Palmer offered invaluable expert advice and volunteer assistance. Jennifer Beatty, James Boldizsar, David Bruer, Andy Carroll, Patricia Chilton, Marion Chow, and Rosalind Hobart deserve thanks for their involvement.

Teri Degler gives additional thanks to her agent, Lee Davis Creal.

Technical Data

As with most things made by humans, books have an impact on the environment. Bindings, the types of paper used, inks - whatever the choices, they can have a bad or a neutral effect on the health of the planet. Like *The Canadian Green Consumer Guide* and *The Canadian Green Calendar 1991*, this book has been made in a way that tries to lessen harm to the environment.

● The text has been printed on Cavalier Opaque, a recycled paper containing a minimum of 50% pre-consumer de-inked fibres, and at least 5% post-consumer waste. Pre-consumer, or secondary, fibre refers to those odds and ends of paper created during the production process and reused at the paper mill. Post-consumer means a paper product has left the mill, been used, then returned for recycling. A book made of at least 5% post-consumer waste permits a company to use the recycled paper symbol approved by the federal government.

● All inks in the text are biodegradable.

● All media and promotional releases for this book have been printed on recycled paper.

● McClelland & Stewart Inc. is a participant in Trees Ontario, a non-profit foundation established by the Ontario Forestry Association and the Ministry of Natural Resources to administer tree-planting and tree-tending programs in the province. At its Toronto offices McClelland & Stewart also operates an in-house "Blue Box" program for the recycling and re-use of sundry paper waste.

● Boxed shipments of *The Canadian Junior Green Guide* (and all other M&S books) are now sent with non-CFC (chlorofluorocarbon) packing materials. Smaller shipments are being packaged with recyclable newsprint or cardboard.

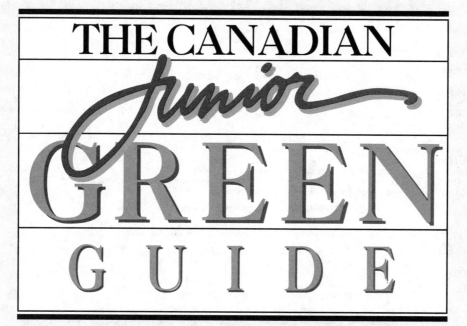

THE CANADIAN
Junior
GREEN
GUIDE

Prepared by
Teri Degler and Pollution Probe

Based on the book by
John Elkington and Julia Hailes with Douglas Hill

Poetry by
Dennis Lee

M&S

Copyright © 1990 by McClelland & Stewart Inc.

To the best of the authors' knowledge and belief the information contained in this book is correct at the time of publication of this edition; but, relying as we do on the good faith of our informants, 100% accuracy cannot be guaranteed over such a wide range of consumer concerns. The authors and publishers will welcome comment on any matter considered to be inaccurate, and upon satisfactory factual and documentary confirmation of the correct position, will use all reasonable endeavours to amend the text for other subsequent imprints or editions. The omission or inclusion of any particular brand, company, or any other organization implies neither censure nor recommendation.

Canadian Cataloguing in Publication Data

Degler, Teri, 1948 - The Canadian junior green guide
Includes bibliographical references. ISBN 0-7710-7157-4

1. Environmental protection - Citizen participation -
Juvenile literature. 2. Man - Influence on nature -
Juvenile literature. I. Pollution Probe.
II. Lee, Dennis, 1939-   . III. Title.
TD171.7. D43 1990   j363.7'0525   C90-095153-2

Based on *The Young Green Consumer Guide* by John Elkington and Julia Hailes with Douglas Hill. First published in Great Britain in 1990 by Victor Gollancz Ltd. Copyright © by John Elkington, Juila Hailes, Douglas Hill 1990.

"Dreaming of Earth," "The Water-Go-Round," "Little Walter Waterdrop," and "Wild!" Copyright © 1990 by Dennis Lee. Used by permission of MGA (Toronto).

"Inspect a pond" (p. 27) from DISCOVERING NATURE by Midas Kedders and Angela de Vrede. Reprinted with permission of Exley Publications, Watford, UK.

"How to clean up an oil spill" (p. 33) reprinted from SCIENCE WORLD Magazine. Copyright © September, 1989 by Scholastic Inc. Permission granted by Scholastic Inc., New York City, NY.

"How to make a solar water cleaner" (p. 39) adapted from **Scienceworks: An Ontario Science Centre Book of Experiments**. Text copyright © 1984 by The Centennial Centre of Science and Technology. Reprinted by permission of Kids Can Press Ltd., Toronto, Canada.

"Make a garbage garden" (p. 69) adapted from **Scienceworks: An Ontario Science Centre Book of Experiments**. Text copyright © 1984 by The Centennial Centre of Science and Technology. Reprinted by permission of Kids Can Press Ltd., Toronto, Canada.

"How to make a draftometer" (p. 71) adapted from **Scienceworks: An Ontario Science Centre Book of Experiments**. Text copyright © 1984 by The Centennial Centre of Science and Technology. Reprinted by permission of Kids Can Press Ltd., Toronto, Canada.

Recipe (p. 77) reprinted from THE SUPER HEROES SUPER HEALTHY COOKBOOK by Mark Saltzman, Judy Garlan and Michele Grodner. Copyright ©1981 DC Comics. All rights reserved. Used by permission.

"Dirtless farming" (p. 101) adapted from **Foodworks: An Ontario Science Centre Book of Experiments**. Text copyright © 1986 by The Centennial Centre of Science and Technology. Reprinted by permission of Kids Can Press Ltd., Toronto, Canada.

Cover and book design: The Watt Group. Cover illustration: Robert Meecham / Joe Weissmann

McClelland & Stewart Inc.
The Canadian Publishers
481 University Avenue
Toronto, Ontario M5G 2E9

Contents

Here's the Green Team

If you're like a lot of young people, you're worried about the environment. You hear about problems like acid rain, holes in the ozone, and the greenhouse effect, and it sounds scary. You wonder what's happening to planet Earth and what things will be like ten years from now.

This book will help you understand exactly what some of the most serious environmental issues are – and show you what you can do to help. These problems are not too big to solve. In fact, most of the big problems have come about because of little things we do every day. This means there is a lot you can do.

THE GREEN
Scientist

THE GREEN
DETECTIVE

This is where the Green Team comes in. The Green Team is made up of people just like you who care about planet Earth.

The Green Scientist: carries out experiments to learn about environmental problems and help find solutions to them.

The Green Detectives: explore nature and use their detective skills to discover the effects of pollution.

The Green Crusaders: take action, write letters to decision-makers, and form groups to fight for change.

The Green Shoppers: use buying power to make even the biggest companies think about the environment.

We all need to be part of the Green Team!

> **The Green Team Reminds You:**
> *When you are doing the projects and experiments in this book, always think SAFETY FIRST. Discuss activities with an adult before you begin!*

THE GREEN CRUSADER

THE GREEN SHOPPER

The Water-Go-Round

Oh, the sea makes the clouds,
  And the clouds make the rain,
And the rain rains down
  On the mighty mountain chain;
Then the silver rivers race
  To the green & easy plain—
Where they hurry, flurry, scurry
  Till they reach the sea again.

(Then the sea makes the clouds,
  And the clouds make the rain…)

Dennis Lee

The Outdoors

Most kids love being outdoors, and many care a lot about animals and plants. But planet Earth – and the plants and animals – are in trouble. In this part of the book, you'll learn what the problems are and how people are causing them.

Some of the problems are very big – they affect the entire earth – yet they are often caused by the little things we do. In a way, this is good news. It means we can begin to solve the problems just by changing some of our everyday habits.

In the following pages you'll learn many interesting and easy ways you can help make things better.

What's Making the Air So Dirty?

Everyone today has heard about air pollution, and most of you know something about it – especially about the kinds that you can see or smell, like the brown smog that hangs in the city air, the dark clouds from a factory smokestack, or the exhaust fumes from a poorly tuned car.

There are also kinds of air pollution you *can't* see or smell. Some of these are poisonous chemicals. Others are naturally occurring gases – like carbon dioxide and ozone – that become harmful only when we create too much of them or when they show up where they are not supposed to be.

Some types of air pollution have natural sources – for instance, the fumes and ashes that a volcano spews into the air or the smoke from a forest fire caused by lightning.

The big problem today, though, is the air pollution made by humans.

The Air

THE THREE WORST AIR POLLUTERS

FACTORIES
CARS
COAL-BURNING POWER PLANTS

■ Some factories burn fossil fuels directly because they need heat to make their products.

■ Other factories use fossil fuels indirectly by consuming electricity from coal-burning power plants.

■ Cars use tremendous amounts of fossil fuels in the forms of gasoline and oil.

■ We heat homes, schools, stores, and factories with fossil fuels in the forms of oil and natural gas.

Getting Dirty...

Really serious air pollution started about 150 years ago, when the first factories were built. These factories belched huge clouds of black, sooty smoke and poisonous gases into the air. Although people could see the "dirt" in the air, most of the world was still unspoiled and clean, so nobody worried about it.

Dirtier...

The next stage in serious air pollution occurred when the automobile was invented. In the early 1900s there were only a few cars in the entire world. Before too long there were millions of cars. When gasoline is burned to run a car's engine, a lot of harmful material is released. The air was getting dirtier.

Air pollution also became worse as people used more and more electricity. Many power stations burn coal to make electricity. A great deal of electricity is used by factories when they manufacture goods. Families use a lot in their homes, too. We have electric everything these days – even electric can openers!

Really, how hard is it to open a can by hand?

Dirtiest...

Now we use – and throw away – more things from factories than ever before. We drive cars more than ever before. We use more electricity than ever before. And the air? It's *dirtier* than ever before!

We have electric everything these days!

How It All Relates to Energy

Most of our energy is produced when we burn fossil fuels. Fossil fuels began to form millions of years ago when dead plants and animals rotted and were covered, over a long, long time, by layers of dirt and more dead plants and animals. As the years went by, heat and pressure changed all this rotting matter into the fossil fuels – coal, oil, and natural gas.

The worst sources of air pollution all burn fossil fuels to release energy.

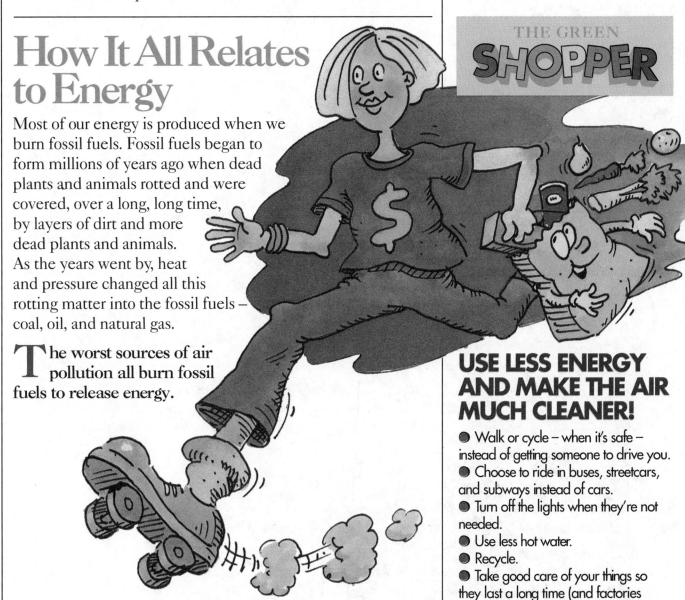

THE GREEN SHOPPER

USE LESS ENERGY AND MAKE THE AIR MUCH CLEANER!

● Walk or cycle – when it's safe – instead of getting someone to drive you.
● Choose to ride in buses, streetcars, and subways instead of cars.
● Turn off the lights when they're not needed.
● Use less hot water.
● Recycle.
● Take good care of your things so they last a long time (and factories won't have to make new ones).
● Don't buy things you don't need.

How Air Pollution Is Harmful

☞ It can cause allergies or make them worse.

☞ It can cause lung and breathing problems, such as asthma, or make them worse.

☞ It harms plants.

☞ It can make farmers' harvests much smaller.

B·A·D NEWS

All this is pretty bad news. But we can't close down factories – they produce things we need, like clothes, or that make our lives more enjoyable. Cars are very convenient. The same is true of most things that run on electricity, from microwaves to stereos and VCRs.

GOOD NEWS

But it's pretty good news too, because – with just a little effort – we can all use much less energy. And every time we choose to use less energy, we make the air cleaner and the planet greener.

Success Story

JANUARY 1, 1990 – A GREEN DAY FOR THE WORLD!

Lead is very poisonous. In Canada it used to be added to gasoline. The lead came out in the car exhaust and the particles hung in the air, where people breathed them in. Green activists in Canada worked hard to tell people how harmful the lead was.

The Canadian government listened. It passed a law saying gasoline now had to be lead-free! The law went into effect on January 1, 1990.

DISCOVER THE AMOUNT OF POLLUTION MADE BY TINY PARTICLES (called particulate pollution) FLOATING IN THE AIR IN YOUR NEIGHBOURHOOD, HOME, OR SCHOOL.

THE GREEN DETECTIVE

What You Need:

➤➤ petroleum jelly
➤➤ an equal number of small jars and large cans (cans should have both ends removed)
➤➤ stick-on labels and a pen

Before You Start:

➤➤ With an adult, choose a few spots in your neighbourhood, home, or school where you'd like to check the level of particulate pollution. Also select one or two places where you think the air is clean. You'll put your jars in those places, so stay away from dangerous areas.

➤➤ Make a simple map of the area and mark on it the spots you chose. Number the spots.

➤➤ Mark your map with things you think might cause particulate pollution. Look for smokestacks, traffic, construction sites, barbecues, fireplaces and chimneys, and incinerators.

What You Do:

➤➤ Rub a heavy coat of petroleum jelly on the outside of the jars.
➤➤ Place the jars upside down at the different spots on your map. Cover each jar with a can. Label each can with the number on your map. Put some jars at different heights.
➤➤ If you place your jars outside, you'll have to cover them or bring them indoors when you think it's going to rain.

After One Week:

➤➤ Collect the jars.
➤➤ Look at each jar through a magnifying glass. What do you see?
➤➤ Where do you think the different particles came from?
➤➤ Which particles seem to come from nature?
➤➤ Which ones seem to be produced by people's activities or by machines?
➤➤ Did the things you thought might cause particulate pollution really do so? Why or why not?

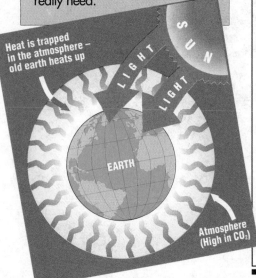

Heat is trapped in the atmosphere – old earth heats up

SUN

LIGHT

LIGHT

EARTH

Atmosphere (High in CO_2)

The Greenhouse Effect

I f you've ever been in a greenhouse, you know it's warm inside even on a cold winter day. The greenhouse isn't heated by gas or oil like our houses; it's heated by the sun. The sun's light rays come through the glass and turn into heat rays. Because heat rays are shaped differently than light rays, they can't get back out through the glass as easily, so most of the heat stays trapped inside the greenhouse. The same thing happens in a parked car on a sunny day.

Warming Our Planet

Our planet is heated in much the same way. The sun shines through the gases in the earth's atmosphere and warms the air. Those gases act like the glass in the greenhouse and trap some of the heat close to the earth. The most important of these gases is carbon dioxide, or CO_2. When the right amount of CO_2 is in the atmosphere, just the right amount of heat escapes. But when there's too much CO_2, not enough heat escapes.

Too Much CO_2

And that's the problem. People are putting too much CO_2 into the air, mainly by burning too many fossil fuels.

Most scientists believe that all this extra CO_2 is going to cause the world to get warmer. Many say the trend has already started. They call it the greenhouse effect – or global warming.

A Warmer Earth – Wouldn't That Be Good?

Most of us – especially many of us living in Canada – would like to see the world warmed up a bit. We'd like to see spring start sooner and have summer last longer.

The trouble is that making the earth warmer could cause some serious problems. Even if the average temperature went up only 1°C, some of the ice at the North and South poles might melt and raise the level of the oceans. Cities and towns on low-lying coasts and islands could be flooded. A lot of land would be buried under water, and birds and animals that make their homes on the water's edge would drown.

The ocean's currents would change, and this would cause changes in the weather. There might be flooding rains in some areas and terrible droughts in others, even in farming areas. People – as well as many kinds of plants, trees, and animals – would die.

A Big Experiment

The truth is, we really don't know what will happen if the earth's temperature rises. There has probably not been much change in the average temperature while humans have been on the earth. So it's a little like we're part of a big science experiment. But Planet Earth is the lab – and we're the guinea pigs!

A lot of people don't like this idea. They're working to stop the greenhouse effect before it gets worse. And you can too.

BURNING DOWN THE TROPICAL RAINFORESTS

A BAD THING TIMES TWO

● Huge areas of rainforest – what we sometimes call jungle – are being burned down every year in places like Brazil. They are being burned down in massive fires to make room for cattle-grazing land.

● This is bad for two reasons. It destroys millions and millions of trees needed to absorb CO_2. And burning trees is like burning fossil fuel – it puts great amounts of CO_2 into the air. All this contributes to global warming.

THE GREEN
Scientist

Question

How can planting trees fight the greenhouse effect?

Answer

- Humans breathe in oxygen and breathe out carbon dioxide. All plants – including trees – take in carbon dioxide and give off oxygen. Trees need some oxygen to live, but they make much more than they need.

- So trees are helpful in two ways. They make oxygen for us, and they take CO_2 out of the air.

- A growing tree can take in as much as 22 kg of CO_2 in a year.

- The more trees we have, the less chance there is of the earth warming up. Plant trees and take care of the trees we have!

We Use Trees to Make Paper

■ It takes about 20,000 trees to make the Saturday edition of a big-city newspaper. That's more than a million trees in a year – and more than 22 000 000 kg of CO_2!

■ Recycling paper saves other trees from being cut down.

**SAVE TREES BY USING LESS PAPER!
SAVE TREES BY RECYCLING!**

The Greenhouse Gases

Other gases besides CO_2 contribute to the greenhouse effect.

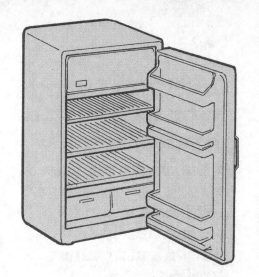

● **Methane** comes mainly from rotting plants and animals, which is why it's found around garbage dumps. It is also one of the gases produced by humans and animals when they digest food – cattle and termites give off a great deal of this gas!

● **Nitrous oxide** comes mainly from burning fossil fuels and is made when fertilizers mix with water.

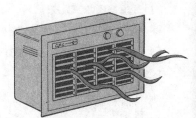

● **CFCs** – chlorofluorocarbons – are gases made by people. They are found mainly in air conditioners and refrigerators and in the manufacture of some plastic foam products such as some of the cups and containers you get in fast food restaurants and foam plastic toys and cushions.

GOOD NEWS FOR THE GREEN SHOPPER

If you've decided to use less energy and clean up the air by doing the things listed on page 11 – like walking and cycling instead of taking a car – you are already helping to stop the greenhouse effect!

CFCs are found in or used in the production of:

● the plastic foam used in some egg cartons and fast food containers
● foam fillings for pillows and furniture
● refrigerator and freezer coolants
● air conditioners
● some foam home insulations

Oh No! Holes in the Ozone Layer!

There has been a lot of talk recently about holes in the ozone layer. But what is the ozone layer? How can there be holes in it? And what does it mean to you?

Ozone is a sharp-smelling colourless gas. A layer of ozone floats in the upper atmosphere, about 20 to 50 km above the earth's surface. It is extremely important to life on the earth because it filters out 99% of the sun's harmful rays. ☞ Continued on page 19

THE GREEN SHOPPER

CAN PROTECT THE OZONE

● It takes up to a hundred years for CFCs to disappear from the atmosphere – so it's important to stop using them right now!
● Don't buy food that comes in plastic foam packages.
● Ask your parents not to buy meat or vegetables in stores that put these foods on plastic foam trays.
● Choose eggs in cardboard cartons – or better yet, help your parents shop in stores where you can reuse egg cartons.
● Remind your parents to take good care of refrigerators, freezers, and air conditioners. Make sure they're checked every year for leaks – such leaks are one of the main ways CFCs get into the atmosphere.

These harmful rays are called UV – or ultraviolet – rays. UV rays can hurt our skin. If you've ever had a bad sunburn you've had a painful taste of just what UV rays can do! Too many UV rays can cause skin cancer and eye diseases. They can do terrible damage to crops and other plants – especially some of the ocean plants that sea creatures depend on for food.

Scientists have found two holes in the ozone layer. One is over the South Pole, and another is over the North Pole. Their size and shape constantly change. It's clear that these holes are a very bad thing, because the UV rays can pass right through them. We know that the biggest cause of these holes is CFCs, a family of gases made by humans.

These holes are getting a lot of attention. And that's good. But the real problem is that the ozone layer is getting thinner *everywhere*. The holes are spots where the most ozone has broken down.

Success Story

*C*FCs were once used in many aerosol spray cans, but when Canadians realized how bad they were, that use was banned in this country in 1978! But lots of CFCs were still being used in other ways. Then in 1987, 30 countries signed an agreement called the Montreal Protocol. They all agreed that, by the year 2000, they would cut the use of CFCs in half. Many people thought this wouldn't help enough. So the countries got together and decided they wouldn't be making *any* more CFCs by the year 2000.

THE GREEN CRUSADER

FIGHT CFCs!

◼ Write letters to fridge and air-conditioner manufacturers to ask them to stop using CFCs now. (You can get the addresses from the warranties or manuals.)

◼ Write to the head offices of fast food chains and find out if they are using paper or reusable dishes. If they use plastic foam dishes or packaging, don't eat there! They'll get the message.

Acid Rain

Acid can be pretty powerful stuff. And the idea of acid coming down in the rain can be scary. Kids sometimes wonder if falling acid rain will burn their skin or burn holes in their clothes. The acid in acid rain isn't strong enough to do those things – but it *is* strong enough to harm the environment. Many people are working hard to get rid of it. You can do a lot to help, too.

Acid Rain Hurts:

● *Trees*
Acid rain weakens trees so they catch diseases more easily and sometimes die.

● *Soil*
Acid rain robs nutrients from the ground so that plants and trees can't grow.

● *Statues and buildings*
Acid rain eats away at some stonework and metals.

● *Lakes*
Plants, frogs, and bugs die in the lakes when the water has too much acid in it.

● *Fish*
Baby fish die in the acid lakes and older fish stop having babies. Soon *all* the fish are gone.

● *Birds and animals*
The ones that get food from the lakes and streams have nothing to eat once all the water life is killed by acid rain. They move away – or starve.

● *People*
Acid rain harms people. It can add dangerous metals to the water we drink.

Burning coal to make electricity is one of the main causes of acid rain. Recycling is a good way to save electricity!

With the same amount of electricity you can make:

one sheet of new paper	**OR**	two sheets of recycled paper
one new glass bottle	**OR**	three recycled bottles
one new aluminum can	**OR**	ten recycled cans

THE GREEN DETECTIVE

FIND OUT HOW MUCH ACID IS IN THE RAIN THAT FALLS WHERE YOU LIVE.

What You Need:

➤➤ a clean wide-mouthed jar
➤➤ narrow-range universal litmus paper (your teacher can tell you where to get a kit)
➤➤ the chart that comes with the litmus paper

What You Do:

➤➤ Set the jar outside, well away from tree branches and buildings.
➤➤ When it rains, make a note of which way the wind is blowing.
➤➤ After the rainfall, dip the litmus paper into the water.
➤➤ Check the litmus paper against the chart in your kit.
➤➤ How acidic is the rain? Compare it to the values on the Acidity Chart.

Things to Think About:

➤➤ What direction did the wind come from during the rainfall?
➤➤ Does that tell you something about what put the acid pollution into the air?

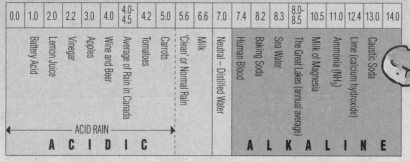

Acidity Chart

0.0	1.0	2.0	2.2	3.0	4.0	4.0-4.5	4.2	5.0	5.6	6.6	7.0	7.4	8.2	8.3	8.0-8.5	10.5	11.0	12.4	13.0	14.0
Battery Acid		Lemon Juice	Vinegar	Apples	Wine and Beer	Average of Rain in Canada	Tomatoes	Carrots	Milk	'Clean' or Normal Rain	Neutral – Distilled Water	Human Blood	Baking Soda	Sea Water	The Great Lakes (annual average)	Milk of Magnesia	Ammonia (NH_3)	Lime (calcium hydroxide)	Caustic Soda	

◄— ACID RAIN —►

A C I D I C   A L K A L I N E

What Is Acid Rain?

Acid rain is a form of air pollution. It comes mainly from smelters, pulp mills, trucks, cars, and coal-burning power plants. Smelters are places where metals like nickel and copper are extracted from rock. Pulp mills make paper. Smelting and paper-making give off a gas called sulphur dioxide. When trucks' and cars' engines work, they give off a family of gases called nitrogen oxides. Coal-burning power plants give off both these polluting gases.

These gases float high into the air and may travel hundreds or even thousands of kilometres on the wind. They mix with the water in clouds and make two kinds of acid – sulphuric acid and nitric acid.

These acids fall to the ground in many forms. Some are wet, like rain, snow, fog, and dew. Some are dry, like little particles of dust, which can drift down to the ground on a bright, sunny day.

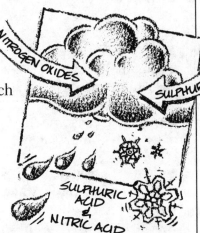

Even though these acids are mild, they cause trouble when they build up in the water and soil year after year.

THE GREEN
DETECTIVE

HOW DO YOU RECOGNIZE TREES THAT HAVE BEEN HURT BY ACID RAIN?

Look for:
➤ bare branches at the top of the tree
➤ leaves that are a funny colour
➤ trees that don't have as many leaves as they should
➤ trees that lose their leaves earlier and earlier each fall

22

THE GREEN
Scientist

FIND OUT WHAT
ACID DOES TO PLANTS.

What You Need:

- two squares of cotton cloth, like a rag or a napkin
- two clear glass jars
- water
- vinegar
- radish or carrot seeds
- sand
- plastic bag
- two rubber bands

What You Do:

- Dampen the cloth with water. Water is not an acid.
- Carefully line the inside of one jar with the cloth.
- Gently peel the cloth back and scatter seeds on it.
- Pat the cloth back against the sides so the seeds are stuck against the sides of the jar.
- Gently pour sand into the jar to hold the cloth in place.
- Cover the jar with a plastic bag and hold it in place with a rubber band.
- Repeat the above steps, but this time moisten the cloth with vinegar. Vinegar is an acid.
- Label the jars so you know which has water and which has vinegar. Put the jars in a darkened area until they begin to sprout. Then move them to where they get some light but not direct sunlight.
- Observe the seeds for two weeks. Apply water or vinegar occasionally to keep the cloth moist.

After Two Weeks:

- What happens to the seeds in water?
- What happens to the seeds in vinegar?
- What does this tell you about the effect of acid ‹and acid rain› on plants?

When Water Isn't Clean

When water becomes too polluted, we cannot drink it or swim in it. Often water plants, fish, and other water animals die. Sometimes the fish live, but they are sick, and we can't eat them because their bodies contain harmful chemicals. But the birds and other animals that live in and near the water don't know this. They eat the fish and can become sick too.

The Main Kinds of Water Pollution

Too Many Chemicals

● Many of the chemicals that get in the water make people and animals sick. Some even kill the fish and water animals.

● Some of these chemicals are called toxic wastes. "Toxic" means poisonous. They are often "waste" – what is left over once many of the things we use every day are made.

Too Much Harmful Bacteria

● Not all bacteria are harmful. But the kinds that are can cause very serious illnesses and diseases.

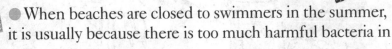

● Human sewage that is dumped straight in to the water, without first being treated, contains harmful bacteria.

● When beaches are closed to swimmers in the summer, it is usually because there is too much harmful bacteria in the water. Continued on page 26

Chemicals can get into the water from:
● manufacturing some plastics
● mining some metals
● making paper
● spraying pesticides on farms and in gardens

GROUNDWATER is water that is found deep in the earth under many layers of rock and sand. Much of the drinking supply for people around the world comes from groundwater. Groundwater gets polluted by toxic chemicals that escape from dump sites, by pesticides and fertilizers used on farms and in gardens, by poisonous chemicals that spill in accidents, and by oil and gas that leak from buried storage tanks. Salt sprayed on roads and sidewalks in the winter also pollutes the groundwater.

THROWAWAY THINGS

Throwaway things are just too easy to pitch in the garbage. They've got three strikes against them. And they're OUT!

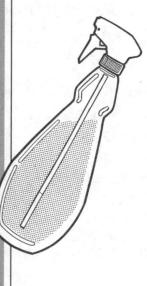

STRIKE ONE

Throwaway things are often made from plastic, and making plastic can pollute the water. Often they come packaged in plastic or extra paper too. Making packaging uses energy and can put toxic chemicals into the water.

STRIKE TWO

Factories make lots and lots of throwaway things – because we keep buying them, using them once, and throwing them away! This uses a tremendous amount of electricity.

STRIKE THREE

Throwaway things make mountains of garbage when we throw them away! This garbage is a problem because we are running out of space for dumps.

THE GREEN

KNOWS

"BUY! BUY! BUY!"
CAN MEAN
"BYE-BYE-EARTH"

- Stop buying things you don't need.
- Stop buying so much throwaway stuff; buy instead items you can reuse.
- Stop buying things that come in too much packaging.
- Stop buying snack foods and desserts that come in one-serving packages.

Some things that deplete the oxygen in the water by rotting or by making algae grow

● Animal Manure, Human Sewage, Vegetable Scraps

Most of these come from cities, towns, and cottages when they dump their sewage and garbage directly into the water.

● Phosphates

Most come from human sewage; they are also found in many powdered dishwasher detergents; some industries dump them in the water.

● Nitrates

These are found in human and animal wastes, and in fertilizers used on lawns and farms.

Not Enough Oxygen

● One kind of water pollution doesn't kill things – it makes some things grow, especially small plants called algae. Only it makes them multiply much too quickly.

● The water then becomes thick with algae. As the algae die, they cover the bottom and rot. When things rot they use up a lot of oxygen.

● This robs the water of the oxygen that fish and other water animals need to live. Soon they die.

Too Much Heat

● Making water too hot is a form of pollution.

● Nuclear and other power plants and some industries can do this.

● They use the cool water from lakes or rivers to cool their equipment, and this makes the water hot. They then dump it back into the lake.

● Some kinds of algae grow more quickly in the warm water.

● Some fish need cool, clear water and can't live in the warmer water.

THE GREEN CRUSADER

ORGANIZE A STREAM OR BEACH CLEANUP!

■ Ask some of your friends to help fight water pollution by cleaning up the litter along a stream or beach near your houses or school.

■ Get a parent or teacher to come with you. This is important! Even streams that look safe can be dangerous!

■ Pick up all the garbage you can find beside the water. Ask the adult to pick up broken glass, jagged metal, used needles and other unsafe garbage you may find.

■ Return bottles for a refund and separate the things you can recycle from the things you need to put in the garbage.

THE GREEN DETECTIVE

INSPECT A POND FOR POLLUTION.

You can find out whether a pond near your home or school is polluted by inspecting the creatures in it. This activity is based on one found in a book called *Discovering Nature*.

Before You Start:

➤➤ Get permission to go to the pond. If you are not allowed to go alone, ask an adult to go with you.

What You Need:

➤➤ a clear or white bowl
➤➤ a fine mesh net

What You Do:

➤➤ Dip your bowl in the pond so it's about half full of water.
➤➤ Scoop the pond with your net and put what you catch into the bowl.
➤➤ Inspect what you see.
➤➤ Scoop up some more. Try getting some mud too.

What to Look For:

Here are some creatures you will find in clean water:

➤➤ Mayflies
➤➤ Caddis-fly larvae
➤➤ Shrimps (they can live in a little more pollution than mayflies)

The water is polluted if you find:

➤➤ Lots of water lice
➤➤ Tubifex
➤➤ Bloodworms

If the water is very polluted, it will sometimes smell bad. But not all kinds of pollution smell bad. Some dangerous chemicals have no smell at all.

If the water is *really* polluted, you won't find any living things at all.

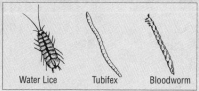

| Mayfly | Caddisfly | Shrimp |

Clean water

| Water Lice | Tubifex | Bloodworm |

Polluted water

The Ocean's Blue

Some pretty sad things have been happening to the oceans and the animals that live in them. But it's not too late to fix a lot of the damage if we all start working together *right now*.

The Oceans as Garbage Dumps

The oceans and seas are so big that people used to think they could dump garbage and other waste in them without doing any harm. Today, we know this isn't true. Yet some industries, cities, countries – and even individuals – still use the waterways as great big garbage dumps. Some waste is dumped directly into the oceans. Other pollutants are poured into lakes and rivers. All rivers eventually empty into the sea, carrying much of that pollution with them.

Human Sewage and Other Wastes

Some cities and towns dump their untreated sewage right into oceans, or into the rivers leading to them. This puts harmful bacteria in the water. It also causes too much algae to grow.

Other things that "fertilize" the algae – like nitrates and phosphates – are carried from towns and farms by the rivers into the ocean.

THE GREEN CRUSADER

What You Can Do

■ Find out what your city or town does with its sewage.
■ If it is dumped untreated into the waterways, write a letter to your local council and complain.
■ Talk with your parents about the problem. Encourage them to vote in the next election for a candidate who is committed to cleaning up the environment.
■ Help your parents with the laundry – and make sure they use pure soap, not a detergent that contains polluting phosphates.

Chemical Pollution

Pesticides, other chemicals, and nuclear waste are all making their way into the oceans. Some are dumped there on purpose by industries, and others are spilled in shipping accidents. Pesticides used on farms and gardens eventually make their way into rivers and are carried to the seas and oceans. And some of the pollution carried in the air can settle in the ocean.

These poisons may be killing the fish and sea animals – and they are certainly making them weaker so that it's hard for them to fight off diseases. The pollution in the fish may even harm us when we eat them.

Plastic Bags and Rings

A lot of plastic gets dumped with garbage into oceans, lakes, and rivers. This also happens when boaters throw their garbage in the water or when litter is left on beaches.

Shopping bags, garbage bags, and plastic rings that go around six-packs of pop cause a big problem in the oceans. Sea turtles and other animals think the plastic bags are jellyfish and swallow them. This often kills them. Sea turtles, dolphins, fish, and seals get the plastic rings caught on their noses, necks, and flippers. They can't get the rings off, and they usually die.

THE GREEN SHOPPER

● Help your parents with the lawn and garden. Encourage them to use natural fertilizer like compost and not to use toxic pesticides!

● Remember, making plastic and paper puts a lot of pollution in the water. So buy fewer things wrapped in plastic or extra paper and avoid plastic foam.

● Watch what you dump down the sink – it may end up in the ocean!

● Buy pop in large reusable or recyclable bottles instead of in six-packs held together by plastic rings.

● If you do get drinks in plastic rings, carefully cut the plastic up and throw it away in the garbage.

Driftnets and Other Problems

Driftnets are huge fishing nets that hang 5 to 15 m deep and stretch through the ocean for as far as 65 km! They are made of very fine clear plastic that fish and other sea creatures can't see and that cannot be detected by dolphins' sonar.

The trouble with driftnets is that they catch and tangle up everything that swims into them – not just the kinds of fish the fishermen want to catch. Thousands and thousands of fish are caught in the nets; if they're not the right kind, they're just thrown back into the sea. Most die. This is a terrible waste because our oceans are already getting low on fish. As well, dolphins, seals, whales, sea turtles, birds, and many other creatures get caught in these nets. These animals suffer and almost always die.

The driftnets sometimes break away from the fishing boats and float off through the sea. Known as ghost nets, these loose nets kill thousands of creatures every year.

GOOD NEWS The United Nations General Assembly has asked countries that use driftnets to show that such nets are not harmful. In 1992, it may request countries to stop using driftnets altogether.

THE GREEN CRUSADER

HELP STOP DRIFTNETS!

Write letters to the Ministry of External Affairs and the Department of Fisheries and Oceans in Ottawa. Tell the minister you want Canada to use the UN resolution to stop driftnet fishing and to encourage other countries to do the same.

Dolphins are being killed by tuna fishermen in the eastern part of the tropical Pacific. There the tuna fishermen watch for schools of dolphins because they know that tuna like to swim just beneath them. The fishermen then wrap a net around the dolphins and the tuna. The dolphins rip their noses and flippers as they try to escape from the net and die when they are hauled out with the tuna.

Three big tuna companies have been listening to the concerns of people who care about the dolphins. They are now buying tuna caught only with nets that don't hurt the dolphins.

HOORAY FOR THESE COMPANIES!

*STAR-KIST

*BUMBLE BEE

*CHICKEN OF THE SEA

THE GREEN
SHOPPER

● Don't buy tuna unless it comes from these three companies. *Don't eat any other kinds.*

● Write letters to the "dolphin-safe" companies and tell them how much you appreciate what they have done.

● Write letters to other tuna companies and tell them you won't buy their tuna until they stop using driftnets or trapping dolphins along with tuna. Your parents or a teacher can help you find the addresses at the library.

Oil Spills

Oil spills happen when ships carrying oil spring leaks or run aground. One of the worst oil spills ever occurred off the Alaska coast in 1989 and dumped more than 40 million L of oil into the ocean. The oil coats animals, such as sea otters, and the many seabirds and often kills them. Animals and birds also accidentally swallow the oil, which poisons them. Some of the oil sinks to the bottom and gets into the food supply. It washes up on the beaches and covers them with thick, oily sludge.

Oil spills are disasters. Yet even more oil gets into the water every year when the tanks on the big oil tankers are cleaned out – and the oily water is dumped into harbours.

OIL SPILLS ARE DISASTERS.

THE GREEN
CRUSADER

■ Write a letter to the Department of the Environment in Ottawa.
■ Tell them you want all oil tankers coming into Canada to have double hulls. The double-hull tankers have an airspace between the two hulls that could prevent the oil from spilling into the water in case of an accident.

single hull

double hull

THE GREEN DETECTIVE

HOW HARD IS IT TO CLEAN UP AN OIL SPILL?

(This experiment is based on one that appeared in the magazine *Science World* in September 1989.)

What You Need for the Oil Spill:

➤➤ pie plates
➤➤ water
➤➤ cooking oil
➤➤ drinking straws

What You Need for the Cleanup:

➤➤ small pieces of different kinds of cloth
➤➤ spoons
➤➤ drinking straws
➤➤ cotton balls
➤➤ string
➤➤ dish detergent (about 10 drops)
➤➤ any other material you think might clean up the oil

What You Do:

➤➤ Fill the pie plates about one-third full with water and "spill" some oil on top.
➤➤ Experiment with the cleaning materials. Try to scoop, soak, or suck up oil.
➤➤ Make new "oil spills" as needed.
➤➤ Keep track of how long it takes you to clean up the oil with each method. Estimate how much of the oil you are able to clean up with each

method, and make a note if the method doesn't work at all.
➤➤ Simulate a storm at sea by having one person blow through a straw to make waves. While the "storm" is raging, try each method again.

Things to Think About:

➤➤ What problems did you encounter?
➤➤ What happens to the oil as time goes on?
➤➤ What does the detergent do? How is this different from the other methods?
➤➤ How hard do you think it would be to clean up an oil spill in the ocean?
➤➤ Is it important to get the oil cleaned up quickly? Why or why not?
➤➤ What happens to the oil when a storm comes up?
➤➤ What's better – cleanup or prevention?

The Canadian North

Canada's North is a special place. It covers both the Yukon and the Northwest Territories and spreads across the top of seven provinces. It is a land of ice, snow, rocks, lakes, and, above the treeline, barren tundra that stretches from coast to coast.

It is a beautiful place, but winter is long and cold. Plants and animals have to make the most of the very short summers. Colourful flowers spring up and scatter their seeds in just a few weeks. Animals give birth to their babies and raise them in the few months before the snow begins to fall again.

The North is home to many rare and fascinating animals and plants: polar bears, muskox, wolves, Arctic foxes and hares, huge herds of caribou, and millions of birds that fly from faraway places just to nest. Whales, seals, and walruses live in the Arctic seas.

The North is also home to native Indians and the Inuit. A few native people still survive by hunting, trapping, and fishing.

In some ways the North is a harsh land, but it is also delicate. It can be easily harmed.

SOME THINGS THAT CAN HARM THE NORTH

❄ Too much mining, drilling, and looking for oil and gas.

❄ Spills from oil tankers and pipelines.

❄ Garbage, empty oil drums, abandoned buildings.

❄ Overhunting.

❄ Scarring of the land by bulldozers and other big machines. Even a human footprint can stay on the ground for decades in the cold, dry Arctic air.

❄ Pipelines that interfere with animals' migration.

❄ Noisy aircraft that scare animals, causing mothers to abandon their babies.

CANADA'S NORTH   THE TREE LINE   CONTINENTAL ZONE

Long Live the Whales

W hales are not fish. They are mammals – warm-blooded animals that produce milk for their babies. Some whales are the largest animals on the planet, and they are very smart. They take good care of their families and get along well with other whales.

Whales live in all the world's oceans. Many once lived successfully in Canada's Arctic waters. For the Inuit, hunting the smaller whales was always a natural part of life in the North. But beginning in the 1600s, other nations joined the hunt, killing millions of whales. By the beginning of this century people were killing so many that whales were in danger of disappearing off the face of the earth forever.

CARIBOU IN TROUBLE

Caribou are another beautiful northern animal, but some herds are in danger. The oil and gas pipelines spoil their habitat and can block their way when they try to migrate. Poisonous chemicals are building up in the bodies of caribou – and other Arctic animals such as polar bears. Some scientists think the wind carries these chemicals from garbage incinerators, power plants, and factories thousands of kilometres away.

B·A·D NEWS Some countries are still hunting whales. Most types of whales have disappeared from the Arctic.

GOOD NEWS People from around the world are fighting to save the whales.

Whale hunting has been banned by agreements involving many countries. It may be too late to save some species, but if we all keep trying we will be able to save many. With luck their numbers will grow again!

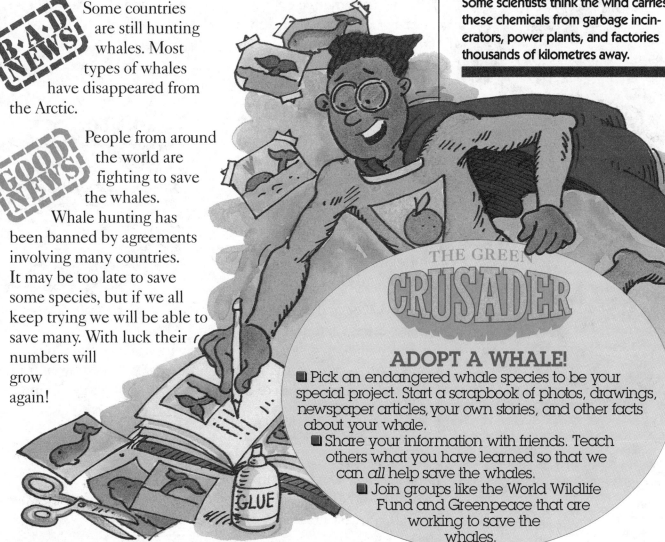

THE GREEN CRUSADER

ADOPT A WHALE!

◼ Pick an endangered whale species to be your special project. Start a scrapbook of photos, drawings, newspaper articles, your own stories, and other facts about your whale.

◼ Share your information with friends. Teach others what you have learned so that we can *all* help save the whales.

◼ Join groups like the World Wildlife Fund and Greenpeace that are working to save the whales.

New Sources of Energy

We don't *have* to burn fossil fuels to get energy (and in the process pollute our planet). We do have some other choices. One is to conserve energy. Another is to use more "alternative" or "renewable" energy sources. We could easily use one-quarter less electricity by being careful not to waste energy and by using things – from lightbulbs to refrigerators – that have been designed to use energy more efficiently.

But will alternative energy be able to provide all the energy we need? Let's see what a few of the most promising sources have to offer.

Solar Energy

Energy from the sun is safe. It's clean. And it won't ever run out. Only a small percentage of the sun's energy actually falls on the earth, but that's more than enough to heat the planet and grow all the crops.

Solar power could be used for many energy needs. For instance, many people now heat their homes with it. Heating homes and water is, in fact, the most common use of solar power. It can also be used to run cars. A few people are already driving solar-powered cars.

Some problems with large-scale solar power production haven't been solved yet. One is that a solar power plant that makes electricity takes up a lot of room – much more room than the other kinds of power plants we use today. Maybe you will be one of the scientists to solve this problem!

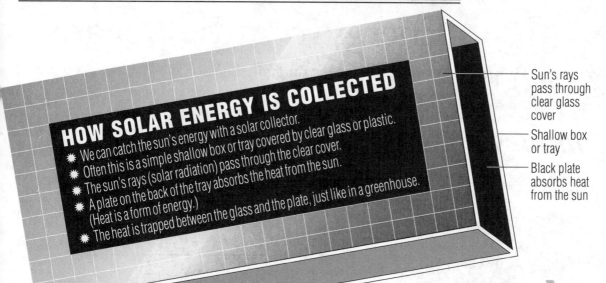

HOW SOLAR ENERGY IS COLLECTED

* We can catch the sun's energy with a solar collector.
* Often this is a simple shallow box or tray covered by clear glass or plastic.
* The sun's rays (solar radiation) pass through the clear cover.
* A plate on the back of the tray absorbs the heat from the sun. (Heat is a form of energy.)
* The heat is trapped between the glass and the plate, just like in a greenhouse.

Sun's rays pass through clear glass cover

Shallow box or tray

Black plate absorbs heat from the sun

Wind Energy

People have been harnessing the wind and using its energy to pump water for centuries. We quit using so many windmills when it became so easy to burn fossil fuels. Now people who care about the environment are working on better ways to harness wind power and use it to run electrical generators. Two problems with these new wind power plants are that they need a lot of room and they can be very noisy. Engineers are working on better windmill designs that will solve both these problems.

Energy from Plants

Biomass is the name we give to energy stored in plants. Trees, for example, store energy and then give it off as heat when wood is burned. Many people around the world rely on this kind of biomass energy to warm their homes and cook their food. Biomass energy can also be turned into fuels such as alcohol and methane, which can be used for heating and to run cars and other motors.

The major problem with biomass energy is that it takes a lot of room to grow the large number of plants that are needed. However, scraps from plants used in other ways can be a source of energy. For instance, after the corn has been scraped off them and used for food, corn cobs can be turned into fuel.

Windmills were used in Persia as early as 200 B.C. In the Middle Ages, the Crusaders learned about windmills during their travels and took the idea back to Europe. Before long the Dutch were building their famous windmills – and by the late 1800s there were about 24,000 windmills in northern Europe!

Energy from the Oceans

Scientists have been thinking about a way to tap the energy of the ocean waves and tides. One way would be to build dams across bays or places where rivers flow into the sea. The water behind the dam would rise as the tide rose. Then the water could be let out to turn generators and make power.

The big problem with this idea is that the dams would cause floods where many animals and birds now make their homes and nests.

Saving energy means saving money.

THE GREEN

SHOPPER

WHAT YOU CAN DO:

- Some gas and electric companies offer free energy audits.
- This means they will inspect your home and tell you how you can use less energy.
- Check with your parents before you arrange to have a free energy audit. They will probably like the idea – saving energy means saving money.
- When it's time to buy a big appliance, like a new fridge or stove, help your parents shop. Compare Energuide labels and pick an appliance that's going to save the most energy.

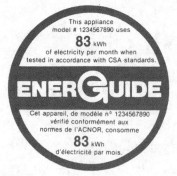

This appliance
model # 1234567890 uses
83 kWh
of electricity per month when
tested in accordance with CSA standards.

ENER⊖UIDE

Cet appareil, de modèle n° 1234567890
vérifié conformément aux
normes de l'ACNOR, consomme
83 kWh
d'électricité par mois.

Nuclear Power

Some people think nuclear power is great because it provides energy without making acid rain or adding to the greenhouse effect. Unfortunately, nuclear power plants leave a waste – called radioactive waste – that is very harmful to living things. And this waste lasts for tens of thousands of years – longer than the whole recorded history of people! We don't know where or how this dangerous waste can be stored, and we have no way to get rid of it.

As well, some serious accidents at nuclear power plants have spilled radioactive waste into the air and water. Nevertheless, more nuclear power plants are being built all the time.

THE GREEN Scientist

MAKE A SOLAR WATER CLEANER!

Use solar energy to clean the dirt out of dirty water. This experiment is based on one from Scienceworks.

What You Need:

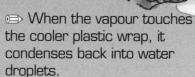 a tub or a very big pan

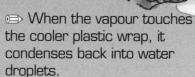 a glass that isn't as high as the pan

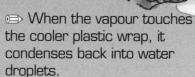 a few small rocks

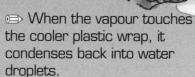 plastic wrap big enough to fit over the pan

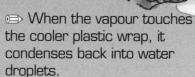 masking tape

What You Do:

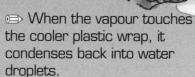 Put about 5 cm of muddy water in the pan.

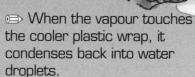 Put the pan in a place where the sun shines all day.

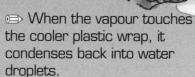 Set the glass in the middle of the pan. If it floats, put one or two clean rocks in it to hold it down.

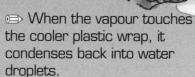 Stretch the plastic wrap over the pan. Make sure it's stretched tight and tape it down.

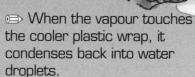 Put a small rock in the centre of the plastic – right over the middle of the glass. It should make the plastic slope gently but not touch the glass.

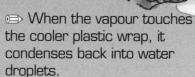 During the day, watch what happens.

How It Works:

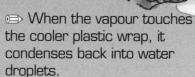 The heat – energy – from the sun warms the water and turns it into vapour.

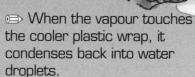 When the vapour touches the cooler plastic wrap, it condenses back into water droplets.

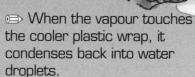 The water droplets collect and roll down the plastic and into the glass.

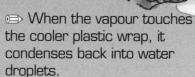 The mud and dirt are left in the pan because they don't evaporate at the same rate as water.

 This process involves evaporation and condensation. It is a way of separating water from dirt and other impurities.

THE GREEN Scientist

FIND OUT HOW TREES WORK LIKE AIR CONDITIONERS THROUGH A PROCESS CALLED TRANSPIRATION.

What You Do:
- Get a large, clear plastic bag.
- Tie it around some leaves on a tree.
- After an hour or two, remove and check the bag.
- Is there water on the inside of the bag?
- The water "transpired" through the leaves.

How It Works:
- Water inside the tree travels to the leaves.
- The water then comes out little holes in the leaves and evaporates into the air.
- When water evaporates it changes from a liquid to a gas. This change uses up heat energy and so the process takes heat out of the air.
- Many air conditioners evaporate water in just this way to cool the air.
- A big tree on a hot day can "transpire" many litres of water.

Trees *(Now That's Green)*

Everybody knows that trees are green. But did you know that when it comes to being good for the environment, they are just about the "greenest" things around?

Here are just some of the ways trees benefit the planet and people:

● Trees produce food. Some bear nuts and fruits, like walnuts, apples, and bananas, that people eat. And all trees have seeds, which are eaten by birds, squirrels, and many other creatures. Some animals, such as deer, eat twigs and buds off trees. In many countries, leaves are used as fodder to feed cattle.

● Trees provide homes for many animals. Birds, chipmunks, and squirrels make nests in trees. Animals such as opossums and raccoons like to live in hollowed-out trunks.

● Trees help people breathe. They take carbon dioxide out of the air and give off oxygen. People breathe in oxygen and breathe out carbon dioxide.

● Trees store carbon in their wood. This reduces the impact of the greenhouse effect as long as the tree is alive.

● Trees take some kinds of pollution right out of the air.

● Trees make shade – and their shade is cooler than the shade a building makes! Trees work just like natural air conditioners. A group of trees growing together can cool the air near them as much as 6°C. Houses with shade trees around them use much less energy for air conditioning – sometimes half as much. (And in winter they're protected from cold winds.)

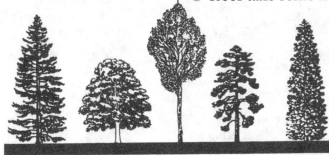

Douglas Fir   Oak   Silver Birch   Jack Pine   Spruce

- Trees planted as windbreaks prevent topsoil from being blown off farmland.
- Trees help prevent floods. Their roots help the ground act like a big sponge, soaking up rainwater and releasing it slowly.

Trees Are Excellent to Have Around

All this sounds great. So what's the problem? The problem is that we are cutting down too many trees too quickly. And we are not planting nearly enough to make up for it. Cutting down trees causes a lot of problems.

- Once the tree is cut down, it can't soak up any more CO_2 or make any more oxygen for us.

- When the tree is destroyed by burning, CO_2 is released – and that adds to the greenhouse effect.

- After the trees are gone, the topsoil erodes – it gets blown or washed away. The soil that's left is no longer good for growing things.

- When trees are cut down, their roots no longer help the ground soak up rainwater – and floods can occur.

Why Are People Cutting Down So Many Trees?

Many trees are cut down in Canada for lumber, but far more are used to make pulp and paper. Most North Americans use more than 260 kg of paper a year. This means the paper that a family of four throws away in a year weighs as much as a car.

Trees are also being killed – or weakened – by acid rain. Trees in cities are often made sick by air pollution, mostly from car and truck exhaust.

How to Plant a Tree

● Buy a seedling at a good nursery. (Choose one that doesn't use pesticides.) Sometimes the local government gives them out free. Call and ask.

● Find a big open space for your tree where there is good light and good drainage. Stay well away from buildings. Look up and make sure the tree won't touch any wires when it grows large.

● With a shovel, loosen the soil around the place you're going to plant your tree. Dig a hole two times as wide as the seedling's root ball and just as deep as the root ball.

● Gently put the tree in the hole and spread out the roots. Be sure they are not tangled or twisted around each other.

● Fill the hole with dirt. Pack it lightly around the roots.

● Spread mulch 5 to 10 cm thick around the tree.

● Put a stake about 30 cm away from the tree. Attach it to the tree with a soft piece of rubber. The tree must be able to flex in the wind. (After six months you can remove the stake.)

● Water the tree well, but don't flood it. Water it twice a week when the weather is dry.

THE GREEN CRUSADER

▢ Organize a group at your school or in your neighbourhood to plant trees.
▢ Invite someone from a local nursery or tree-planting group to come and talk to your group.
▢ Plant a tree in your yard too!
▢ Take good care of the trees you plant. Water them. Spread compost around them in the spring.
▢ Write letters to local businesses and ask them to plant trees on their property.
▢ Get a teacher to help you organize a fine paper recycling program at your school.
▢ Make sure your family recycles its newspapers.

A Living Christmas Tree

Many nurseries will sell your family a living, potted Christmas tree that can be replanted outdoors after the holidays, year after year. A small evergreen tree, less than 1.5 m tall, can be brought indoors for up to two weeks without harming it. Store the soil you'll need for replanting the tree in a warm place so it won't freeze.

TREE PLANTING HINTS

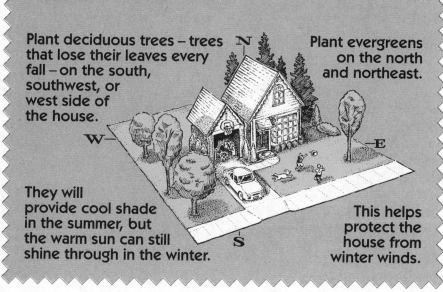

Plant deciduous trees – trees that lose their leaves every fall – on the south, southwest, or west side of the house.

Plant evergreens on the north and northeast.

They will provide cool shade in the summer, but the warm sun can still shine through in the winter.

This helps protect the house from winter winds.

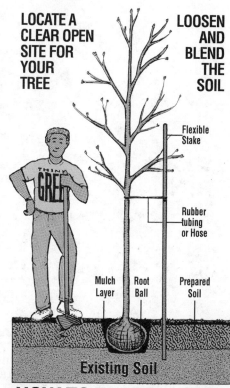

LOCATE A CLEAR OPEN SITE FOR YOUR TREE

LOOSEN AND BLEND THE SOIL

Flexible Stake

Rubber tubing or Hose

Mulch Layer

Root Ball

Prepared Soil

Existing Soil

HOW TO PLANT A TREE

Saving the Tropical Rainforests

The tropical rainforests grow in a belt around the equator. They are the thick, lush forests we sometimes call jungles. The biggest tropical rainforest is around the Amazon River in Brazil. Other rainforests of this type grow in Africa, Asia, and parts of Australia.

THE EQUATOR'S TROPICAL RAINFOREST BELT

Millions upon millions of birds, animals, and insects make their homes in the rainforests. In fact, half of all the living things on Earth live in rainforests. They are also filled with wonderful tropical plants, which are not only beautiful but useful – many medicines can be made from them. And many native people have lived in the rainforests for generations.

We desperately need the trees in the rainforests to produce the oxygen we breathe and to take CO_2 out of the air, helping prevent the greenhouse effect. These rainforests generate about 40% of the world's oxygen.

But the rainforests are being destroyed at an alarming rate. The people who live there have nowhere to go, and many rare and fascinating animals, like gorillas, tropical birds, tigers, and monkeys, are dying. This terrible situation is made even worse because much of the rainforest is being burned down – and that puts more CO_2 in the air!

THE GREEN CRUSADER

Protect an Acre of Rainforest!

■ You can send $25 to the World Wildlife Fund and ask them to use it to protect an acre of rainforest for you.

■ The World Wildlife Fund uses the money to turn an acre of rainforest into protected land, to take care of parklands already set up, to educate people about preserving the rainforest, and to work with native people from the rainforest to find out more about how valuable the plants and animals there are.

■ You can send the money in as a gift for someone's birthday. Then they'll be the one helping the rainforest!

■ Look in the back of this book for the addresses of the World Wildlife Fund and The Children's Rainforest Program.

The Rainforests Are Being Cut and Burned Down for Four Main Reasons...

1 **Large multinational companies are cutting down the forest for wood.**

● This wood, such as teak and mahogany, is called tropical hardwood.

● It is used in everything from doors and furniture to throwaway chopsticks.

2 **The forests are being burned down to make room for beef cattle.**

● Not much of the beef is used to feed the people in these countries. Instead, it is sent to wealthy countries like Britain, Canada, and the United States.

● It is used in fast food hamburgers, hot dogs, TV dinners, and pet food.

● The forest soil is not rich. Enough grass to feed cattle will grow on it only for one or two years. Then the ranchers must move on and burn down more rainforest.

3 **The forests are being flooded behind huge** hydroelectric dams, which produce electricity.

4 **Some of the forests are being cleared by poor people who have nowhere else to raise food to eat.**

● The people cut or burn down a little bit of forest for a place to grow food.

● But the soil isn't good, so after a year or two they have to move on and clear more forest.

● These people can't use the good farmland because much of it is taken up by huge plantations that grow coffee and other crops sold to wealthy countries like our own.

THE GREEN SHOPPER
WHAT YOU CAN DO

● Don't buy things made of tropical hardwoods, and ask others not to either.

● Find out where fast food chains buy their hamburger. Don't buy food there if they get their beef from rainforest land.

● A lot of rainforest beef is packaged as corned beef and canned meat products.

● Cook meals without meat! Learn how you can eat less meat and still be healthy.

Farming the Land

There are more people on the earth than ever before – and so we need to grow more food than ever before. Modern farming methods have made it possible for us to grow far more food than we did in the past. But modern farming also causes some problems for the environment.

Pesticides and Fertilizers

Pesticides are chemicals we put on crops to kill pests – insects, plant diseases, and weeds that harm crops.

The problem with pesticides is that they kill many helpful creatures, too – ones that eat pests, pollinate flowers, and actually *help* the crops grow. People can get sick if they breathe in pesticides.

Fertilizers make plants grow faster. Cow and horse manure are examples of natural fertilizers. This used to be the only kind of fertilizer that farmers used. But now powerful chemical fertilizers have been developed.

When fertilizer is put on the fields, it doesn't all get used up by the crops. The leftovers get washed into streams, rivers, and lakes.

Chemical fertilizers often contain nitrates. These make the algae in the water grow too quickly and die. They decompose and use up too much oxygen, which causes fish and other water creatures to die.

It is important to wash pesticides off your fruits and vegetables before you eat them.

THE GREEN DETECTIVE

The Search for Rich Soil!

Topsoil is the rich earth that plants grow in. If you have ever looked in a freshly dug hole or along a riverbank, you may have noticed the topsoil. It is usually dark and crumbly. In some places it is only a few centimetres thick. In other places it might go down a metre or so. It is full of plant roots. The dirt under the topsoil is a much lighter colour, and there aren't many roots in it.

What makes the topsoil so rich and good for plants? Here's how you can find out.

➵Get an adult to go with you on a walk in the woods or in a park where the leaves aren't raked.

➵Take a magnifying glass with you.

➵Walk on leaves under the trees. Trees once produced these leaves by taking nutrients out of the soil.

➵Now the leaves lie like a thick carpet on the ground. Check to see how thick it is.

➵How thick would it be if all the leaves that fell off the trees every year were still there? Where *are* all those leaves? What could have happened to them?

➵Dig down into the leaves. Look at their undersides with your magnifying glass.

➵Do you see long, stringy white threads? Or any tangled-up ones?

➵These are moulds. Bacteria and moulds make the leaves rot. The rotting goes on for a long time and breaks the leaves down into smaller and smaller bits.

➵Now check to see what the soil looks like under the leaves. Is there a thick black gooey layer before you get to the dirt? This is humus.

➵Where could the humus come from?

➵If you guessed that humus is made out of the leaves, you're right!

➵The humus now contains all the nutrients that were once in the leaves.

➵Over time the humus becomes part of the soil and makes it rich – ready to grow more trees!

THE GREEN

Scientist

NATURE IS SO SMART!

The rich topsoil – needed for growing plants – is protected by the very plants that grow in it. The roots of trees and plants prevent erosion – that means they keep the topsoil from getting blown away by wind or washed away by rain.

Here's an experiment you can do to see how nature prevents erosion.

What You Need:

- two 22x28 cm cake pans
- a big sprinkling can filled with water
- some dirt
- a piece of sod – dirt with the grass and weeds still growing in it

What You Do:

- Fill one pan with dirt. Pack it down a little.
- Get an adult to help you cut a piece of sod the size of the other pan. Put the sod into the pan.
- Use blocks or bricks to tilt the pans so the dirt and sod seem like they are on a hill.
- Make a "rain" run down the "hill" by pouring water from the sprinkling can onto the plain dirt.
- What happens to the dirt?
- Now do the same thing on the sod.
- What happens to the dirt here?
- How does nature protect the topsoil from erosion?
- What kinds of things would be bad for the topsoil?

When the Soil Isn't Rich

Most farms used to produce many different crops. But modern farms tend to specialize, which means they grow one kind of crop. This is bad for the land because growing the same crop all the time robs the soil of nutrients. So farmers have to use more fertilizer. Plants that grow in the nutrient-low soil are weak. So farmers have to use more pesticides to protect them.

More fertilizers and pesticides also have to be used when farmers try to grow crops on land that isn't really good for farming. This happens a lot in developing countries, where people are cutting down forests for farmland.

This is a very difficult problem! Everyone wants farmers to be able to grow more food. But no one is happy about using more pesticides and fertilizers.

GOOD NEWS People have been afraid that if we don't use pesticides and fertilizers we won't be able to grow enough food for the world's population. But some studies show that using fewer pesticides might help us grow more food! And this would certainly help the environment.

More and more farmers are running organic farms – where only natural pest controls and fertilizers are used. As a Green Shopper you can support organic farming. See page 00!

Save the Animals

We get so used to thinking of ourselves as people that often we forget that we are *animals* too. Humans are just one of the many thousands of plant and animal species that live on this Earth. But sometimes we are not very good at sharing the planet. Many kinds of plants and animals are being cruelly treated by humans, and others are becoming extinct.

SMALL THINGS IN THE BIG PLAN

The small living things may be more important than you think. All life is connected in delicate balances called ecosystems.

There are so many different life forms that no one knows for sure what each one does – or how important it may be. Some of them become extinct before we ever have a chance to find out.

Many plants are important for medicine. Right now, one out of every ten prescription medicines comes, at least in part, from a plant. We might be losing plants that would cure diseases or provide food for the world's hungry. We might be losing tiny creatures that are important – in some way we don't yet know – for the life cycle of the creatures we already know and love.

Going, Going, Gone

When an animal becomes extinct, it is gone forever. No more of its kind will ever exist again. Extinction is a natural process. Ever since animals and plants first appeared on Earth, they have been evolving or changing. As some developed and survived, others died out. In fact, nine out of every ten species that ever lived on Earth are now extinct.

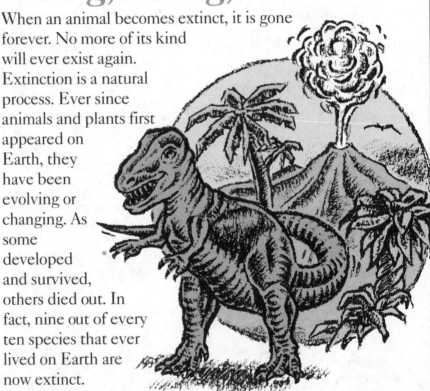

Usually it takes millions of years for a species to die out. Unfortunately, humans are causing a lot of species to die out much more quickly. A hundred years ago, about one species a year became extinct. Now we lose at least one species *a day*! That's too many! Some scientists say that – if you count all the plants, insects, and extremely small creatures – as many as 45 kinds of living things become extinct each day.

Animal Action!

We are in danger of losing animals we care about, like whales, parrots, tigers, monkeys, rhinoceroses, elephants, sea turtles, gorillas, and many, many more! A lot of Canadian animals, such as beluga whales, cougars, wolverines, and sea otters, are threatened, too.

But don't despair! You can help save these animals. First, you need to know what causes the extinctions. In Canada, the main causes are pollution and loss of habitat. Overhunting and bringing new species into an area are two other things that endanger animals the world over.

LOSS OF HABITAT

A habitat is an animal's home. It includes all the land it needs to hunt, gather food, find a mate, and raise a family. If an animal's habitat is destroyed, the animal can't survive in that area. This even includes humans.

Wilderness habitats – from forests and wetlands – are often destroyed when they are logged to get lumber, mined for metals or coal, flooded behind dams, or built over with homes, shopping malls, factories, garbage dumps, and farms.

POLLUTION

Poisons that get into the soil or water can wipe out whole species of animals. The beluga whales that swim in the St. Lawrence River are in serious danger because of all the pollution people dump into the river.

Saving the Wetlands

W*etlands are bogs, swamps, and marshes. They are a very important part of ecosystems.*

● They are the habitats for many plant and animal species.

● Coastal wetlands are needed by a great many birds, fish, and shrimp for laying eggs and raising young.

● Wetlands provide a buffer against floods.

● Rice is a wetland crop. Billions of people rely on rice for food.

● In some places wetlands make excellent grazing land during the dry seasons.

● Wetlands remove some kinds of pollution from the water!

The world's wetlands are being destroyed rapidly. They are drained, turned into farmland or housing projects, or made into reservoirs for power dams.

Canadian Endangered Species

○ Bowhead whale
○ Eastern cougar
○ Eastern wolverine
○ Right whale
○ St Lawrence River beluga whale
○ Sea otter
○ Ungava Bay beluga whale
○ Vancouver Island marmot

Canadian Threatened Species

○ Eastmain beluga whale
○ Maritime woodland caribou
○ Newfoundland pine marten
○ North Pacific humpback whale
○ Peary caribou
○ Prairie long-tailed weasel
○ Wood bison

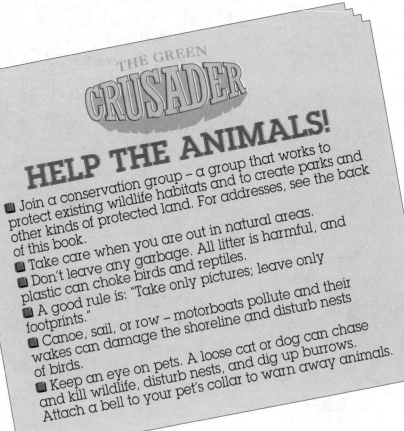

THE GREEN CRUSADER

HELP THE ANIMALS!

■ Join a conservation group – a group that works to protect existing wildlife habitats and to create parks and other kinds of protected land. For addresses, see the back of this book.

■ Take care when you are out in natural areas.

■ Don't leave any garbage. All litter is harmful, and plastic can choke birds and reptiles.

■ A good rule is: "Take only pictures; leave only footprints."

■ Canoe, sail, or row – motorboats pollute and their wakes can damage the shoreline and disturb nests of birds.

■ Keep an eye on pets. A loose cat or dog can chase and kill wildlife, disturb nests, and dig up burrows. Attach a bell to your pet's collar to warn away animals.

Some Canadian Endangered Animals

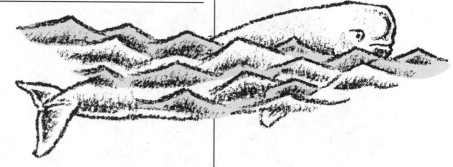

St. Lawrence River Beluga Whale

● These are white, medium-sized whales.

● Once there were more than 5,000 of these whales – now there are only a few hundred.

● Pollution being dumped in the St. Lawrence is making the whales sick and killing them.

● Scientists have found more poisons in these whales' bodies than in any other whale in the world.

● The World Wildlife Fund and Greenpeace have been urging people to clean up the St. Lawrence River. Now Environment Canada is developing a plan to help.

Sea Otter

● The sea otter is one of the most playful of all animals.

● Overhunting once caused them to disappear completely from Canadian waters. Now they are back!

● But they are still in danger from oil spills.

● If there are no more serious oil spills in their habitat, the sea otter may be taken off the endangered species list in a few years!

Success Story

THE WOOD BISON

The dark, woolly wood bison was taken off the endangered list in 1988. The wood bison population declined because of overhunting and bad winters, and they were once thought to be extinct. Then some were found in 1958. Although they are not completely out of danger yet, the World Wildlife Fund has been working very hard to save them.

Eastern Cougar

● The Eastern cougar is a very big cat! Some adults weigh over 100 kg and are more than 2 m long!

● This animal is shy and good at hiding. Very little is known about it.

● But we do know there are few left. The cougar population has been drastically reduced by overhunting.

● Now biologists want to find out more about the Eastern cougar so they can help save it from extinction.

Eastern Wolverine

● The Eastern wolverine was put on the endangered species list in 1989.

● It is a feisty, curious, and bold animal, about the size of a chubby cocker spaniel.

● The Eastern wolverine is in trouble because its habitat and some of the animals it eats are disappearing. Trapping is also a threat.

● Making sure Canada has plenty of wilderness areas will help save the wolverine.

THE GREEN CRUSADER

Some animals and plants are endangered because they, or products made from them, have been exported for sale. It's such a problem that some countries signed a special treaty to discourage this trade. The treaty is called the Convention on Trade in Endangered Species of Flora and Fauna. Canada is a member, and it has an office in Ottawa. You may write to this office for information.

CITES
Canadian Wildlife Service
Place Vincent Massey
Ottawa, Ontario K1A 0E7

Success Story

THE WHITE PELICAN

The white pelican was the first animal to be taken off the Canadian endangered species list, in 1987. It is still not completely out of danger, but many things have helped save it:

✳ *The ban on DDT, a dangerous pesticide that can no longer be used;*

✳ *Better preservation of its habitat;*

✳ *People being more careful not to disturb its nesting sites.*

Much of the work to save the white pelican was sponsored by an insurance company called Canada Life.

Animals in Trouble Around the World

Elephants

● About ten years ago there were one and a half million African elephants. Today there may be only about 400,000 left.

● They are in danger because poachers – illegal hunters – are killing them for their ivory tusks.

● The ivory is being made into jewellery, carvings, ceremonial dagger handles, and ornaments.

● The elephants also don't have enough space because more and more people are attempting to farm more and more land.

Tigers

● There are only about 5,000 tigers left in the wild.

● Tigers are in trouble because too many have been killed to make coats and rugs.

● Their forest homes are being cut down for farmland and villages.

● The World Wildlife Fund has been working hard to help, and the number of tigers is slowly increasing.

Sea Turtles

- Sea turtles have been around since the time of the dinosaurs.

- There are seven species of sea turtles – *all* are endangered.

- Poachers steal their eggs. Some people think it is a great treat to eat turtle eggs and soup.

- Turtle shells are used to make combs and jewellery.

- Plastic bags – garbage from cities and ships – and balloons look like jellyfish. The turtles choke to death when they eat them.

- Scientists and volunteers are helping to save sea turtles by scooping up the eggs before poachers can get them, keeping the eggs until they hatch, and then letting the babies go free.

Giant Pandas

- There are probably no more than 800 to 1,000 giant pandas left in China.

- Giant pandas need bamboo to eat. But the bamboo forests are being chopped down to make room for villages and to grow rice.

- Giant pandas were hunted for their pelts, which were made into sleeping mats. Although hunting giant pandas is now illegal, some are still being poached.

- Twelve giant panda reserves have been set up in China. Scientists are studying their habits to help them survive.

GOOD MAGAZINES TO READ

Subscribe to a good magazine that tells you about nature and animals. Two are *OWL* and *National Geographic World*. Check out the list at the back of this book.

THE GREEN SHOPPER

MANY ENDANGERED SPECIES ARE BEING KILLED FOR THE THINGS THAT ARE MADE FROM THEM.

DON'T BUY

– and tell other people not to buy – anything made from

IVORY • TORTOISE SHELL • CORAL REPTILE SKINS • ANIMAL SKINS

If everyone stops buying these things, there will be no more reason to kill these animals. Most of this is very expensive stuff that you don't have any reason to buy. But often stores for tourists have little trinkets made from parts of endangered animals.

Don't buy anything from stores that sell these items. Tell the store manager why you are not shopping there. You will help save the elephants, the turtles, the crocodiles, the tigers, the leopards, and many more animals in danger!

"DON'T BUY ANYTHING FROM STORES THAT SELL THESE THINGS"

THE GREEN DETECTIVE

TAKE A WALK-AND-STOP WALK!

Excellent detectives use more than just their eyes. They look, listen, sniff, and touch! Take a walk-and-stop walk next time you are in the forest and use your senses. Here's how:

➤➤ Ask an adult to go on the walk with you.

➤➤ Walk into the woods for about 10 minutes.

➤➤ Turn around and start back. But take 25 minutes for the return journey.

➤➤ Walk for a little way and then pause. Use your senses. Look. Smell. Listen. Touch. Keep doing this.

➤➤ What do you find that you didn't notice on the first trip? Bird songs, animals chattering, teeth marks or scratchings on trees, animal or bird tracks, flowers, nests, burrows? What else?

Spaceship Earth

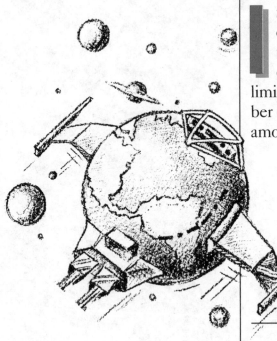

In the 1960s a man named Buckminster Fuller began calling our planet Spaceship Earth. He wanted people to think of the earth as a spaceship travelling through space on a very long journey. He wanted us to realize that there is limited room on the spaceship. It will hold only a certain number of people, other animals, and plants. There is only a certain amount of clean water, clean air, and room for food to grow.

If we acted – all the time – as if we were sailing through the universe on Spaceship Earth, it would be easy to remember:

● to use as little of everything as possible

● to reuse everything as often as possible

● to recycle everything we can.

We Are All in This Together

We should also never forget that each and every living species on the planet is in this together. Everyone and everything is connected on Spaceship Earth. This means the things we do here in Canada affect life all over the world. If we in Canada use more than our share of energy and resources, it means somebody in the world gets less. If we pollute the air or water in Canada, it means we are polluting the whole world's air and water.

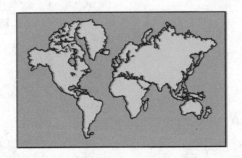

THINK OF THE EARTH AS A SPACESHIP ON A VERY LONG JOURNEY

One of the biggest problems facing Spaceship Earth is hunger. Many children and grownups around the world aren't getting enough to eat. You might be surprised to learn that this problem is connected to the environment.

Famine – a time when there is not enough food to eat – is caused mainly by:

● Poor farming practices and overgrazing that turn good land into desert and make the effects of drought much worse.

● Farmers growing cash crops – coffee, tea, cocoa, cotton, and tobacco – that they can sell to wealthy countries for lots of money instead of growing food for hungry people to eat.

● Many people in the developed (rich) countries getting more food than they need while many people in the developing (poor) countries don't get enough.

● Too many people on the planet.

THE GREEN CRUSADER

HOLD A JUNK-FOOD FAST!

A fast is a time when you don't eat something. Green Crusaders around North America are holding junk-food fasts. Consider doing it yourself! Or get your whole classroom to go on the fast. Promise not to eat any junk food – candy, pop, chips, etc. – on one day a week for a number of months. Then donate the money you would have spent on junk food to an organization that helps solve world hunger or that gives out food in your town or city to people who don't have enough to eat.

HOLD A WASTE WATCH!

Students in some schools have made a bet with local businesses. The bet is whether all the students who eat in the school cafeteria can be careful enough about not wasting food that there is less than 500 g of garbage at the end of lunchtime. Each day that the students win the bet, the businesses donate a certain amount of money to help fight world hunger.

THE GREEN
SHOPPER

SHOP AND EAT LOW ON THE FOOD CHAIN

The expression "eating low on the food chain" means to eat more fruits, vegetables, and grains – corn, wheat, oats, and rice – than meat and dairy products.

◉ Corn, wheat, and rice are the most important sources of food in the world.

◉ The average North American uses up *four* times as much of these foods as a person in a developing country does.

◉ People in the developing countries eat their rice, wheat, or corn directly.

◉ But in North America people eat a great deal of meat, eggs, and milk. Cows, chickens, and so on first eat the wheat or corn and then turn it into the meat, eggs, and milk for the people.

◉ This is not the most efficient way to use grain! The grain used to feed livestock in Canada, the U.S, and Europe in one year would feed 1 billion more people if it was eaten as grain in the first place.

◉ There are lots of delicious and nutritious ways to use grains as the main course of a meal.

◉ More and more people are learning to cook and eat this way.

◉ You can too. There are lots of good vegetarian cookbooks in your library or health food store.

Spaceship Earth Is Getting Crowded!

The earth's population reached 5 billion not too long ago. And it will reach 6 billion by the year 2000.

The bigger a population gets, the faster it grows. There are always more and more people having more and more children. No one knows how many people can live on the earth. It depends on how much food we can grow without ruining the environment and endangering other species.

The things that contribute to world hunger – like spreading deserts, big plantations growing cash crops, and overpopulation – work together in a very complex way. The following steps show you – in an overly simple way – how one thing can affect another, and then another, and so on, making the problem worse and worse.

The population increases by about 160 babies a minute – that's more than 233,000 people every day!

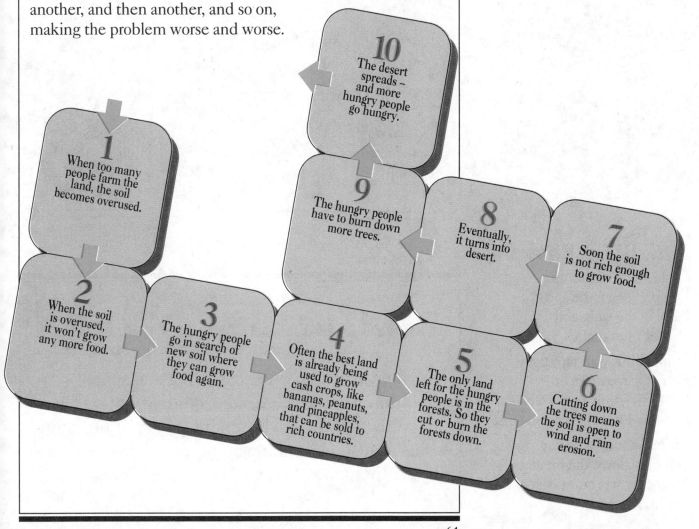

1 When too many people farm the land, the soil becomes overused.

2 When the soil is overused, it won't grow any more food.

3 The hungry people go in search of new soil where they can grow food again.

4 Often the best land is already being used to grow cash crops, like bananas, peanuts, and pineapples, that can be sold to rich countries.

5 The only land left for the hungry people is in the forests. So they cut or burn the forests down.

6 Cutting down the trees means the soil is open to wind and rain erosion.

7 Soon the soil is not rich enough to grow food.

8 Eventually, it turns into desert.

9 The hungry people have to burn down more trees.

10 The desert spreads – and more hungry people go hungry.

Little Walter Waterdrop

Little Walter Waterdrop
Dripped down the spout,
Plop! in the sink, and
He began to shout:

"People, shut your taps tight!
Do not leave them on—
For I was happy in my tap,
But now I've dripped and gone!"...

Little Walter Waterdrop
Dribbled down the drain,
And never will our washroom ever
See his like again.

Dennis Lee

Home and School

The way we do things at home and school—from what we eat to the sports we play—has an effect on the environment. Many of the things we use cause pollution when they are made, when we use them, or when we throw them away.

The good news is that we can learn to be kinder to the environment in everything we do. We can even celebrate our holidays, care for our pets, and choose clothes in ways that are easier on planet Earth. And we can have a great time doing it! Learning to "Think Green" may mean we have to change the way we do some things, but it certainly doesn't mean we need to have less fun!

Waste –
What a Waste!

The average Canadian throws away a tonne of garbage a year! That's about equal to the weight of a small car.

ONE TONNE

How many things will you throw away today? If you made a list you'd be amazed! There was the cereal box you finished at breakfast, the throwaway pen you used up at school, the drinking boxes, the pop cans, the chip bags, and the candy wrappers.

And think about snacks! Some come in a big package, but each snack is individually wrapped, too. Often each one is also packed in a little plastic or paper tray. What looked like a great big snack turns out to be a little tiny snack wrapped up in a whole lot of paper and plastic! It's so small you probably have to eat two! *And* throw all that wrapping away!

The average Canadian throws away a tonne of garbage a year! That's about equal to the weight of a small car.
But because the garbage is not compact like a car, it takes up much more room.

Garbage Mountains

Think how many garbage bags full of trash your family throws out each week. Think how fast you'd fill up your house with those bags if nobody came and took them away! All that garbage causes some *big* problems in the environment:

● Garbage dumps – or landfills – are filling up. We are running out of places to put new dumps. Good farmland is being turned into dumps.
● Liquids leak out of dumps and pollute water.
● Poisonous gases are formed in dumps. For example, methane can move through the ground, get in basements, and cause explosions. (Methane is also a greenhouse gas!)

● Incineration – burning garbage – isn't the answer. It can cause air pollution. Also, burning material that could have been recycled is a waste of valuable resources.

B·A·D NEWS

A province the size of Ontario loses over half a hectare – the size of a football field – of good land to make room for garbage *every day*!

GOOD NEWS

Many cities and towns in Canada are having great success with Blue Box recycling. Each family is given a Blue Box to fill up with glass bottles, cans, plastic containers, and other things that can be recycled. The city collects everything from the Blue Boxes, as well as bundled newspapers and cardboard, for recycling. In one Ontario community, East York, 98% of the people started using their Blue Boxes as soon as they got them. The Blue Boxes are much more successful than anyone hoped!

THE GREEN SHOPPER

◐ When you need paper–buy recycled!

◐ It's better if it's not bright white. Some dangerous chemicals are produced when paper is bleached white.

THE GREEN DETECTIVE

HEAVY-DUTY GARBAGE
FIND OUT EXACTLY HOW MUCH GARBAGE YOUR FAMILY PRODUCES.

➤➤ For two weeks, weigh every bag of garbage that leaves your home.

➤➤ Just climb on the scale while holding the bag in your arms.

➤➤ Subtract your weight from the total and you have the weight of the garbage.

➤➤ How much garbage does your family produce in two weeks? In a year? How much does each person make?

➤➤ Now use the same method to find out how much paper your family throws out.

➤➤ Collect and weigh all the newspapers, magazines, and advertising flyers that you get in two weeks.

➤➤ How much does it weigh? Did you know it takes 17 full-grown trees to make only one tonne of newspaper?

➤➤ How many trees would it take to make the paper your family throws out in a year? What if you included things like paper towels, tissues, toilet paper, and notebook paper?

Gads! All That Garbage

AT LEAST ONE-THIRD OF THE TONNE OF GARBAGE EACH CANADIAN MAKES IS FROM PACKAGING!

How does a Canadian kid make a tonne of garbage a year? Most of it comes from cans, bottles, paper, plastic, table scraps, and lawn trimmings. At least one-third of this garbage is packaging!

Packaging protects things and keeps them clean. Sometimes it's necessary – it would sure be hard to buy milk or pop without something to hold it in! But too often packaging is just there to catch our eye – to make us choose one product over another, or to buy something we don't need at all.

Hey Canadian – Your Garbage Weighs a Tonne!

Every year each of us dumps:

125 kg of yard trimmings
75 kg of newspapers
75 kg of other paper
50 kg of food scraps
45 kg of glass
25 kg of metal
25 kg of plastic
15 kg of cardboard
10 kg of wood
10 kg of disposable diapers
10 kg of fine paper (notebooks, letters, magazines)
5 kg of box board (cereal boxes, etc.)
5 kg of clothes and cloth
25 kg of other things

Cans and Metal

Garbage mounts up fast. Take, for instance, a simple thing like cat food cans. Your cat may eat one can of food a day. If your cat lives for 15 years, you will use 5,475 cat food cans! That's 219 kg of steel – more than 40 times what your cat weighs!

Cans, foil wrap, and things like those little throwaway cups that butter tarts come in are made from important metals like aluminum and steel.

Mining the metal ore is bad for the earth, and making these things causes a lot of pollution.

Glass

Long ago anything made of glass was a prized possession. Now it's just garbage! Glass is made mostly from sand – and there's plenty of sand in the world.

But the sand has to be dug up, and that can leave ugly scars on the land. More important, making glass uses up huge amounts of electricity.

Paper

Canadians use the wood from more than 100 million trees every year just to make paper and cardboard for things like newspapers, magazines, junk mail, paper towels, tissues, and boxes.

Making paper uses up energy, pollutes water, and destroys wildlife habitats. All this for things we often don't need!

Plastic

More than 10% of all packaging is plastic. Plastics are made from oil and other fossil fuel resources, which are disappearing. One problem with plastic is that it is not biodegradable – that means it will lay around for years and years in garbage dumps without breaking down. Making it also causes water pollution and uses a lot of energy.

There is a new "biodegradable" plastic, but it isn't the answer. It does break down, but it leaves a plastic dust that may be harmful. And it can't be recycled.

THE GREEN SHOPPER

A lot of things you buy–candy, chocolate bars, gum, and pop–have the _worst_ packaging. That means you can do a lot to help! You can stop eating this stuff. Or:

- Don't buy anything that has extra packaging.
- Tell the store managers and the product makers why you don't buy it.
- Buy things in bulk–many snacks come that way now.
- Buy big containers instead of little ones–there's less waste packaging.
- Buy drinks in returnable bottles–and return them!

FIVE BAD PACKAGES

O·N·E
DRINKING BOXES. They can't be recycled in your Blue Box or at your local recycling depot.

T·W·O
PLASTIC BUBBLE PACKAGES. Cheap toys often come in these. They are a big waste and can't be recycled.

T·H·R·E·E
INDIVIDUALLY WRAPPED FOODS like snacks and salt, ketchup, and sugar at fast food restaurants.

F·O·U·R
PLASTIC FOAM EGG CARTONS. They don't break down in dumps. Cardboard ones work just as well – and can be made from recycled paper.

F·I·V·E
MICROWAVE SNACKS that come in individual servings, throwaway trays, or with extra packaging.

Good Garbage

I t's clear that these great heaps of garbage are getting to be a serious problem. But it's so very easy to do something about it! One way is to stop thinking of garbage as garbage. Start thinking of garbage as something good!

The Three Rs

If you think of garbage as something valuable, it will be easy for you to practise the three Rs. This will be one of the best things you can do for planet Earth!

Reduce

Buy and use less. This doesn't mean you have to suffer! But get only what you *really* need.

Reuse

It's not garbage until you throw it out! Find new and creative uses for old things instead of buying new things.

Recycle

This still uses some energy and resources, but it's much better than making things from scratch.

Remember

REDUCE
REUSE
RECYCLE

THE GREEN

CRUSADER

MAKE A LITTERLESS LUNCH!

▢ Buy a lunch box or bag you are going to reuse many times.
▢ Or make your own reusable bag out of cotton cloth. Sew patches on it of "green" symbols, with endangered species or slogans on them.
▢ Collect containers that you can keep using so you don't have to use plastic wrap for sandwiches and cookies.
▢ Use a refillable drink container. Then you can buy your juice in big bottles or cans – small cans and drinking boxes cause a lot of waste.
▢ Don't buy desserts or snacks that come in single-serving containers.

THE GREEN Scientist

MAKE A GARBAGE GARDEN!

Plant a garden that doesn't grow – it just rots! You can find out what garbage biodegrades – breaks down – and what could be around forever. (Based on an activity in *Scienceworks*.)

What You Need:

- a plastic bag
- a nylon stocking
- a 100% cotton cloth or sock
- a piece of newspaper
- some foil wrap
- an apple core and/or vegetable peelings
- a scrap of wool
- a plastic cup

What You Do:

- Dig a hole about 10 cm deep for each piece of garbage.
- Wet each hole.
- Plant your garbage and cover it with dirt.
- Mark each hole so you know what is buried where.

After 30 Days:

- Dig up the garbage.
- What biodegrades – rots or breaks down – quickly?
- What doesn't?
- What does that tell you about garbage?
- What is okay to bury when you're camping?
- What must you be sure to take out of the woods?

THE GREEN SHOPPER

- BUY THINGS THAT LAST A LONG TIME.
- TAKE CARE OF THEM.
- DON'T BUY THROW-AWAY THINGS.

FINDING GOLD IN YOUR GARBAGE

IS THAT OLD NEWSPAPER GARBAGE?

NO! It's part of a tree that might have taken a hundred years to grow.

IS THAT POP CAN GARBAGE?

NO! It's a valuable piece of aluminum made from bauxite ore that was mined from the earth.

IS THAT BOTTLE GARBAGE?

NO! It's sand that had to be dug out of the ground and melted down with enormous amounts of energy.

Saving Energy

You can do great things for planet Earth by saving energy around the house. We use energy every time we turn on a light, the microwave, a video game, or the furnace. Most appliances, like fridges and washers, use electricity. Natural gas and oil are also used for energy – usually heat – in our homes.

B·A·D NEWS Did you know it takes about 400 kg of coal just to run one 100-watt lightbulb around the clock for a year?

GOOD NEWS That means you can help the earth by just doing a little thing like switching off the lights!

Since energy is consumed to produce the things we use in the home, we can save energy by buying fewer things, taking better care of them, repairing them, and making them last longer.

THE GREEN SHOPPER

TAKE THE UTILITY BILL CHALLENGE!

Your family pays for the energy it uses. Bills for electricity, natural gas, and oil are called utility bills. They come every month or two.

⬤ Next time one of the bills comes, look it over and challenge the whole family to lower the next bill. Decide together how much you think you can save.

⬤ The electricity bill is a good one to try first – since it's easy to stop wasting so much electricity.

⬤ Plan a treat for the whole family if you meet your goal.

SAVE ENERGY AROUND THE HOUSE!

⬤ On sunny winter days, open the drapes to allow the sun to warm the room naturally. On hot summer days, keep the drapes closed to keep the room cooler.

⬤ Use a fan instead of an air conditioner.

⬤ Turn things off – lights, radios, TVs, stereos, computers, VCRs – when you are not using them.

⬤ Keep pots covered and the oven door closed when you're helping with the cooking.

⬤ Use small appliances like toaster ovens and microwaves instead of the big oven.

⬤ Don't stand in front of the fridge with the door open! Decide what you want before you open the door.

⬤ Put on an extra sweater instead of turning up the furnace. Change into shorts and a T-shirt instead of turning on the air conditioner.

THE GREEN DETECTIVE

The Great Heat Escape!

In the winter, warm air escapes from your house and cold air blows in through cracks and small holes that are hard to see. In the summer, cool air escapes and hot air comes in. Drafts of air are a good clue that this is happening. Here's how you can make an instrument to detect drafts around your house.

What You Need:

➤➤ a piece of tissue paper

➤➤ tape

➤➤ a long pencil

What You Do:

➤➤ Tape one edge of the tissue securely to the pencil.

➤➤ Walk around the house holding the pencil to all the windows, doors, and fireplaces.

➤➤ Be sure to check the sides and bottoms of the doors and windows.

➤➤ When the tissue moves like a curtain in the wind you know you've found a draft! That means there are cracks or holes.

➤➤ Help your family plug the leaks.

CHECK THOSE THERMOSTAT SETTINGS!

FURNACE
No higher than 20°C when people are at home, and 17°C at night or when nobody is home.

FRIDGE
FRIDGE: 3°C
FREEZER: -18°C

WATER HEATER:
49°C

Water Down the Drain

Every Canadian dumps about 300 L of water down the drain – every day!

Turn the tap and you've got water. Water is so much a part of our lives that we don't even think about it. We just let it run! We have forgotten that pure, clean water is valuable. Canada's factories and homes use much more water a day than those in most other countries. We use almost six times as much as Britain does – and they have twice as many people!

THE GREEN DETECTIVE

Water's Going Down the Tubes!

That little tap that goes drip, drip, drip in your house can waste up to 30 L of water in one day! The amount of water lost in a leaky toilet could fill the bathtub three times a day! So, find out if your house has any leaks.

➤➤ Check the water meter one day just before everybody leaves for several hours. Write down the numbers from the meter.

➤➤ As soon as you get home, check the meter. Be sure to do it before anyone uses any water. Write down the numbers again.

➤➤ If both sets of numbers are not the same, it means water was used up while you were gone. Where did it go? Leaks!

➤➤ Start hunting for those leaks. Check every faucet in the house. Don't forget to check the outside faucets, too.

➤➤ Next, check the toilet. Get an adult to help you take the lid off the water tank. Put some bright food colouring in the tank. Make sure no one flushes the toilet during your experiment.

➤➤ After a while check the water in the bowl. Has any colouring come through? If so, you've got a leak!

One reason Canadians use so much water is that we *think* it's cheap! That's because the water bills your family pays are low. But these bills don't include the huge cost of cleaning the dirty water. These costs are hidden in the taxes your parents pay. And you have probably heard them say that taxes sure aren't low!

In countries like Switzerland, where water is expensive, people don't waste it. In countries like Canada, where water bills seem cheaper, people are not as careful about how much they use. We need to remember that water is very valuable.

We could easily save a lot of the water we dump down the drain. Almost half of the water we use is flushed down the toilet!

REMEMBER
when you use more hot water than you need, you not only waste water, you also waste the energy required to heat it!

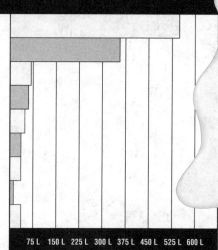

THE GREEN Scientist
SAVE 54 L OF WATER A DAY!

➤ Soak the labels off a plastic jug.

➤ Put some small rocks in it so it won't float.

➤ Fill it with water. Put the top on tight.

➤ Get an adult to help you take the lid off the toilet tank.

➤ Carefully put the jug in the tank so it doesn't touch any of the working mechanisms.

➤ Now each time you flush, you'll use about 10% less water!

HOW TO KEEP WATER FROM GOING DOWN THE DRAIN

● Help your family fix all leaks.

● Always turn taps off tightly.

● Take short showers (less than seven minutes) or shallow baths.

● Don't let the water run continuously when you brush your teeth or help with the dishes.

● Keep a container of drinking water in the fridge rather than running the tap until it's cold.

THIS IS HOW AN AVERAGE FAMILY OF FOUR USES WATER EVERY DAY.

TOILET FLUSHING	540 L	
BATHING	360 L	
KITCHEN	72 L	
DRINKING	60 L	
LAUNDRY	48 L	
CLEANING	36 L	
SPRINKLING	36 L	
CAR WASHING	12 L	
OTHER	36 L	
TOTAL	**1200 L**	75 L 150 L 225 L 300 L 375 L 450 L 525 L 600 L

Write

to the Canadian Wildlife Federation

(the address is at the end of this book) and ask for their free book Recycle for the Birds. *It shows you how to use things like milk cartons to make feeders and homes for birds.*

Really Green Gardens & Lawns

The way we take care of our lawns and gardens can make a big difference to the environment. Perfect lawns may look lovely, but they were probably treated with a lot of chemical fertilizers and pesticides. These may be harmful when they are used on lawns and gardens.

Beautiful lawns and gardens can be grown organically. We just have to change our thinking about exactly what is beautiful. When you were younger you probably thought dandelions were gorgeous, but once you learned they were "just weeds" they didn't seem so pretty any more.

A weed is only a weed because we *say* it is. If we saw the beauty in more so-called weeds, we wouldn't be so frantic to spray them with weed-killers!

THE GREEN DETECTIVE

SOCK WALKS!

➤ Put a big pair of fuzzy, woolly socks over your shoes.

➤ Take a walk through a field on a fall or summer day.

➤ Take off your socks and find out what you've picked up. Look through a magnifying glass.

➤ Plant any seeds you collected in sterile potting soil. Be sure they get sun and water.

➤ Once the plants grow, try to identify them. Library books will help!

Life's Better with Bugs

Did you know that bugs are a necessary part of our lives? They have many important jobs. For example, bees make honey and pollinate flowers, and spiders eat mosquitoes and flies. Some insects in their grub stage, help speed up decay and make valuable humus.

The number of bugs must be kept in balance. Nature does a pretty good job of this. A bird, for instance, can eat close to its weight in bugs in one day! But when birds eat a lot of bugs that have pesticides on them, they can get sick and die. Then we have fewer birds – and more bugs. So people use more pesticides. Then even more birds die. Does this make sense to you?

Encouraging birds to visit your garden is one way to get rid of bugs. Another is to learn about companion planting. Planting onions near carrots, for example, can help keep rust flies off the carrots! And if you *do* have to use a bug spray, you can make organic ones. There are lots of good books that will teach you how to be an organic gardener!

THE GREEN Scientist

ATTRACT WILDLIFE TO YOUR GARDEN

☞ Plan your garden so that you have a variety of plants that flower all through the summer.

☞ Plant large groupings of the same plant.

☞ Wildlife is not attracted to grass.

☞ Squirrels and birds like bushes and trees with berries and seeds.

☞ Hummingbirds like plants with red and yellow flowers.

☞ Butterflies like plants with big, colourful flowers.

☞ All creatures need water – make a birdbath or little pond.

☞ Plant evergreen shrubs and trees to provide winter shelter.

Food Chains and Fast Food Chains

All food chains begin with many small, simple plants like algae and grass. At the other end are the complex animals, like human beings, hawks, and sharks. An animal's place on the food chain is determined by what it eats – and what eats it!

For example, a tiny green plant called plankton floats in the ocean. A small fish eats the plankton, a bigger fish eats the small fish, a bear eats the big fish, a person shoots and eats the bear.

THE GREEN SHOPPER

BUY LOCALLY!

It's always a good idea to buy food that is in season and grown locally. Otherwise it has to be grown in a greenhouse or shipped to you from far away. Heating greenhouses in the winter takes a lot of energy. And the trucks carrying produce across the continent use a lot of fuel.

Even more energy is used to bring such exotic produce as mangoes and kiwis across the ocean! Produce grown locally is fresher and usually tastes better!

Eating Low on the Food Chain

Human beings can choose where they want to eat on the food chain. You are eating "high" on the chain when you eat animals (meat). You are eating "low" on the food chain when you eat plants (fruit, vegetables, grains). Eating low on the food chain is good for you. One reason is that toxic chemicals such as pesticides tend to concentrate – build up – in animals that are high on the chain. There are more of certain pesticides in meat than there are in vegetables and grains.

Also, growing plants for food is much easier on the earth – and much less wasteful – than producing meat. A book called *Diet for a New America* says:

● Raising cattle takes 100 times more water than growing crops.

☞ Continued on page 77

● Producing meat takes up to 20 times more fossil fuels than growing vegetables.

● It takes 20 times more land to grow food for a meat eater than for a vegetarian. This means that lots of trees, sometimes rainforests, must be destroyed to make room for cattle.

People who always eat low on the food chain – who don't eat animals – are called vegetarians. Whenever we eat vegetarian meals, we save land, water, trees, and energy.

If North Americans ate just **10**% less meat, there would be food available for **60** million more people each year. It just so happens that's about the same number of people who **DIE** of hunger in the world each year.

THE GREEN CRUSADER

COOK LOW ON THE FOOD CHAIN!

More and more people are becoming vegetarians or eating much less meat. Here's an excellent meatless recipe you can make with only a little help from an adult. It's from The Super Heroes Super Healthy Cookbook (©1981 DC Comics Inc.).

What You Need (for 4 people)

1 L fresh vegetables (use any combination of carrots, broccoli, peppers, mushrooms, cabbage, zucchini, and/or celery)
1 onion
15 mL vegetable oil
1 mL oregano
1 mL basil
1 mL salt

What You Do:

1. Wash and cut the vegetables. Peel and cut up an onion.
2. Put oil in a pan, add basil, oregano, salt and onion.
3. Put pan over medium heat. Keep stirring with a wooden spoon until onion is soft.
4. Add other vegetables. Keep stirring until they are brightly coloured and soft.

Serve with cooked brown rice.
For every cup of rice, stir in 75 mL of sesame seeds and you have a healthy meal – one that doesn't use meat, eggs, or milk.

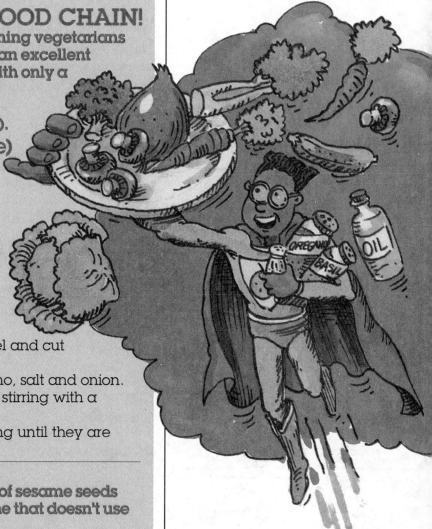

Eating Free-range and Organic

When you think of animals on farms, you probably think of them running happily in the fields. But now many animals are raised on factory farms, where they are packed together in pens or very small cages and have no freedom.

If you don't like the idea of factory farms, you can buy "free-range" meat and eggs. Free-range animals are allowed to be outside and walk around. You can also get organically raised meat. The foods these animals eat don't have chemicals added to them. That means fewer chemicals end up in the environment – and in our bodies!

You can buy organically grown fruits and vegetables too. Look for them in supermarkets or at health food stores. Organic fruits and vegetables often do not look as perfect as ones grown with a lot of chemicals. We have to realize that "perfect" doesn't always mean better. Organic produce may have the odd spot or bug bite, but it's chemical-free, which makes it much better for the environment – and for you! Organic produce sometimes costs a little more, but the price will start to go down when more people buy it.

THE GREEN Scientist

LEARN MORE ABOUT NATURE AND ANIMALS BY MAKING A FOOD CHAIN MOBILE!

What You Need:
- paper and coloured pencils
- scissors, tape, string
- 3 short sticks and 1 longer one

What You Do:
- Have a librarian help you find the books you need.
- Pick a meat-eating animal you are interested in – for instance, a hawk.
- Read about the animal to find one thing it eats. Hawks eat mice.
- Now find one thing a mouse eats – for instance, corn.
- This is a food chain with three things in it: hawks, mice, corn.
- Pick two more animals and make food chains with at least three things in them.
- Draw pictures of all the animals and plants in each chain.
- Make a mobile like the one in the picture.

FAST FOODS AND TAKE-OUTS
Taking a Big Bite Out of the Earth

Fast food and take-out food are fun to eat, but they are really rough on the environment. The biggest problem is the packaging – it causes trouble when it's made and when it's thrown away. And over a hundred thousand tonnes of it end up as garbage every year!

These containers might be handy for keeping your food warm if you're taking it home, but do you need them when you are eating in the restaurant? Loads of napkins, cups, straws, and plastic cutlery are thrown away too. And think of those individual servings of ketchup, salt, pepper, and sugar. What a waste of plastic, paper, and foil. What a lot of garbage!

Why can't all these places give you reusable plates and cutlery when you're eating in? Why can't they use ketchup bottles and sugar bowls?

THE GREEN CRUSADER

ORGANIZE YOUR CLASS OR A GROUP OF FRIENDS TO GO TO A FAST FOOD RESTAURANT FOR A MEAL.

■ Have everybody bring their own reusable plates, cups, and cutlery.

■ Line up and order your food – but ask the servers to put your food on your own dishes. Politely explain that you don't want to make any more garbage.

■ Ask to talk to the manager. Tell him or her that you'd like to be able to have reusable dishes and cutlery when you eat in.

■ If you have a lot of people involved, call the local TV and radio stations – they may want to come down and interview you!

■ A few fast food chains are experimenting with recycling. That's good. But reusable or refillable containers would be the best choice.

Zoos, Marine Parks, and Circuses

When you visit a zoo, be patient. Take time to watch the animals. Let them be themselves. Don't expect them to put on a show for you. Don't throw things or bang on the cages to get their attention.

Some people like zoos because they are places where we can learn about animals we would not otherwise see. Other people *don't* like zoos because the animals are kept in cages and tanks and not in their natural habitats.

Some zoos are better than others. Next time you go to one, use the "Zoo Checklist" to decide how good or how bad the zoo is. If the zoo is very good you'll be able to answer yes to all of the questions.

ZOO CHECKLIST

 CHECK BOXES

- Are the animals kept in large, open enclosures that are as similar as possible to their natural habitat?
- Do the animals have some private space where they can get away from the watching people?
- Are the animals treated with respect and not expected to perform tricks?
- Are visitors provided with information that helps them appreciate the animals more?
- Is the zoo breeding and protecting endangered species and putting them back in the wild?
- Does the zoo make sure visitors do not feed the animals?

THE GREEN CRUSADER

If a zoo isn't treating its animals properly, write to the zoo director about what bothers you. You can also contact a group called Zoocheck, which helps protect animals in zoos and wildlife displays across Canada. They also promote conservation projects.

Zoocheck Canada
5334 Yonge Street
Suite 1830
Toronto, ON
M2N 6M2

Marine Parks

Watching the animals in marine parks can be a lot of fun, and some coastal parks care for injured sea animals. But often the animals are kept in very small enclosures not at all like their natural environment. Although *we* like it when dolphins and whales perform, can we really be sure the animals like it?

Circuses

All the animals in circuses are expected to perform tricks. Some circuses don't take good care of their animals. For example, they keep them in cages that are too small. Some countries, like Switzerland, have regulations that guarantee a certain level of care for animals. But not all Canadian provinces do!

Animals have their place on the planet. We need to treat them with great respect. We should never think they are here just for our entertainment.

Greening Your Pet

A well-cared for, happy pet is a joy! Yet you need to think about a lot of things if you have a pet or if you want to get one.

- There are far too many neglected pets. Humane societies are forced to kill thousands every day.
- If you want a pet, adopt one from a humane society or animal shelter.
- Get your pet neutered or spayed so there won't be any babies.
- Dogs and cats eat a lot of meat, and that puts a strain on the environment. We need to keep the number of pets down.
- Wash your pet with biodegradable shampoos.
- Use natural flea powders.
- Buy pet food and treats in bulk or giant containers to avoid excess packaging.

THE GREEN CRUSADER

WRITE A LETTER TO YOUR PREMIER
to find out about your province's regulations to protect zoo and circus animals. Tell the premier you want strict regulations for animal protection!

THE GREEN SHOPPER

MAKE A NATURAL FLEA COLLAR!

- Rub your pet's collar in oil of pennyroyal once a week.
- Check out your library for lots of other recipes for natural flea remedies.

Be Beautiful... Not Beastly

Are you starting to use things like make-up, hairspray, deodorant, creams, and lotions? Or do you sometimes buy them as presents? If so, here are some things you need to know.

Almost every ingredient in these products has been tested on animals to see if it is safe for human use. More than 17 *million* rabbits, dogs, mice, guinea pigs, and other animals are experimented on every year in North America. The animals suffer terribly during these tests. Many go blind, and they are all killed in the end.

We have to make sure products are safe for people, but testing them on animals is a very controversial method. This is especially true in the case of beauty products. One reason is that beauty products are not essential – we could live just as well without them. Another is that a large selection of "cruelty-free" beauty products is already available. Either these products have not been tested on animals, or their ingredients are already known to be safe. Since there are plenty of these safe ingredients around, many people feel there is no reason to continue to make animals suffer. Also, new cruelty-free safety tests can be done with computers and cells grown in laboratories.

Animal–and Environment –Friendly

Here are some things to think about when you buy bath products and cosmetics:

● Use soaps that don't have fancy perfumes or colourings, which can take a long time to biodegrade.

● Buy recycled toilet paper and tissues. If they're un-bleached too, they're even better.

● Aerosol cans are wasteful because they are only two-thirds filled with the product. Even if they are labelled "ozone friendly," they create excess garbage. A pump spray is a more environment-friendly alternative.

● The best containers are refillable. You can buy the product you like in big bulk containers and refill the smaller ones.

● Always choose items you can use again and again, rather than disposable ones.

● Choose items with the least packaging. For example, an unpackaged bar of soap is far better than liquid soap in a throwaway plastic pump.

● Buy in bulk as often as you can.

THE GREEN CRUSADER

WRITE LETTERS TO THE MAKERS OF PRODUCTS YOU LIKE.

(The addresses are on the containers or packaging.)

ASK: Do they test their products on animals?

❑ Do any of the companies that supply their ingredients test them on animals?

❑ What is in their products? Do they contain substances from animals? (A number of cosmetic companies obtain ingredients from rare and wild animals.)

❑ If you don't like the answers you get, tell the company that, until they change, you are going to switch to products from a cruelty-free company.

THE GREEN SHOPPER

Homemade cleaners are usually much cheaper than the ones you buy. Here's an easy recipe for a good all-purpose cleaner to use on floors, counters, and painted walls. Be sure to have an adult help you.

MIX TOGETHER:

50 mL baking soda
125 mL white vinegar
4 L warm water

Store in a tightly sealed container. Label it (and all homemade cleaners) to prevent accidents!

THE GREEN CRUSADER

NEXT TIME YOUR CLASS, GROUP, OR CLUB WANTS TO SELL SOMETHING

suggest an alternative to the usual candy, cookies, and chocolate. Cloth shopping bags, biodegradable soaps and shampoos, homemade air fresheners, and small houseplants are all good choices.

Clean and Green

The cleaning cupboard in your house is probably filled with liquid cleaners, powders, polishes, and detergents. Most of them contain chemicals that are toxic to people and harmful to the environment. These chemicals get washed down the drain and into our rivers and lakes. Often they end up coming right back out our water taps!

Most of our household cleaning and laundry can be done with three environment-safe cleaners: pure soap, vinegar, and baking soda. Adults may also use borax, ammonia, and washing soda for tough cleaning jobs. Find "recipes" for homemade cleaners in the library and in books like *The Canadian Green Consumer Guide*, and give them to your parents and the cleaning people at your school to use.

Plants-Natural Air Fresheners

Houseplants clean the air and give off fresh oxygen for us to breathe. Scientists found that some plants can even remove a few common pollutants from indoor air. These plants include:

Spider Plants

Aloe Vera

Pot Mums

Golden Pothos

English Ivy

Heart-leaf Philodendron

Getting Around the Greener Way

Cars are one of Canada's biggest sources of air pollution. They make smog and greenhouse gases and contribute to acid rain.

Before you ask for a ride, think! Can you bike, walk, rollerskate, or skateboard instead? If so, do it! If not, take public transportation.

Bikes are one of the most efficient ways to get around. Eating a muffin, an apple, and a glass of milk gives you

muffin + apple + milk

EQUALS ENOUGH ENERGY TO MAKE A 25 KM BIKE TRIP!

enough energy to make a 25 km bike trip. A car consumes more than 50 times that much energy to go the same distance. And the car usually gets energy from gasoline – a polluting and non-renewable resource!

BETTER BIKING EQUALS MORE BIKERS

More and more people will ride their bikes as it becomes safer and more convenient. Write to your city or town hall and campaign for:

- more bicycle paths
- bicycle lanes on busy streets
- more and better bike stands
- sewer grates that won't catch bike wheels
- more public education on the benefits of biking

THE GREEN CRUSADER

ORGANIZE A BIKE-TO-SCHOOL WEEK!

- Ask interested students and teachers to help you.
- Have the school lunchroom cook a pancake breakfast for the bikers.
- Organize a draw with prizes for people who ride. Ask bike shops to donate prizes.
- Have experts on biking give talks and demonstrations on bike safety and maintenance.
- Start a bike-to-school or another type of bicycle club.

Sports and Games

Earth-friendly Fun

Where do you get video games, portable cassette players, toys, and sports gear? From stores? No. From planet Earth. The raw materials that go into making the things you like to have fun with were once part of the earth's natural resources. A lot of energy is also used up in making them. This doesn't mean you have to give up having fun! But it *does* mean two very important things.

ONE You need to choose games and sports gear that will last instead of ones that will break easily and be thrown away.

TWO You need to take good care of what you have so it will last a long time.

When games and toys last, they can be passed down to younger family members – or even to your own kids some day! You can also swap sports stuff, cassettes, computer games, and so on with your friends. That way, when you get tired of things, you don't have to rush out and buy new ones.

Batteries Not Included

It takes a great deal of energy to keep our TVs, computers, and cassette players running. You can save energy by *always* remembering to turn things off when you are not using them.

Batteries are another problem. It takes 50 times more energy to make a battery than that battery will ever provide! A lot of batteries also contain cadmium or mercury – two very toxic metals. More than 2 billion batteries are used up in North America every year. That means a lot of toxic chemicals are put into the environment when batteries are made *and* when they are thrown away.

Be Better about Batteries

- Plug in portable players whenever you can.
- Use rechargeable batteries. But don't waste them – they don't last forever, and many still have cadmium in them.
- Never mix new batteries with old ones. The old ones drain the power out of the new ones.
- Choose things that run on solar power – for example, a solar calculator.
- Whenever you can, choose things that don't require batteries.
- Batteries are hazardous waste. Don't throw them in the garbage. Contact the public works department and ask them where you should dispose of them, or ask the store where you bought them to take them back.

GREENER FUN

Some activities hurt the environment less than others. A walk in the woods, for instance, doesn't require any special equipment, and it doesn't burn any energy but your own! It also helps you feel more a part of the natural world. You can probably think of many other similar activities. Here are a few:

- bird watching
- orienteering
- animal tracking
- plant and animal identification
- hiking
- snowshoeing

The World of BIRDS

THE GREEN DETECTIVE

HOW ENVIRONMENT-FRIENDLY ARE YOUR FAVOURITE ACTIVITIES?

Here are some things to think about: What goes into making the equipment? Does the equipment last a long time? Can you trade used equipment instead of throwing it away? Does the activity cause pollution? Does it damage vegetation or animals? How much energy does the activity use up? (It's okay if it's *your* energy it's using!)

GET YOUR WHOLE CLASS OR FAMILY TO THINK ABOUT THESE ACTIVITIES:

- cycling
- dirt-bike racing
- motorboating
- downhill skiing
- canoeing
- snowmobiling
- ice skating
- kayaking
- football
- cross-country skiing
- baseball
- photography
- snowshoeing
- skateboarding
- water-skiing
- rollerskating

Green Fashion

A lot of people think that having designer labels and wearing the hottest fads makes them cool. Some people even think having expensive clothes is the most important thing on earth. Of course, that's not true. *Having an earth* is more important!

Every single thing we wear causes some environmental problem. Does that mean we should give up clothes? Of course not. But there are some things we can do:

● Buy well-made clothes that last. Take good care of them.

● Don't be a slave to fashion, because you will end up buying more clothes than you need and you won't wear them for very long.

● Be creative with old clothes. Figure out new ways to wear them. Learn how to sew and alter your clothes when new styles come along.

● Don't throw old clothes away. Donate them to charity, wear them for messy projects, or cut them up for quilts, doll clothes, or rags.

CHECK THOSE LABELS!

Clothes made from natural fibres are better than synthetic (made by people) fibres. But there are some problems with them all. Bleaches and dyes used in processing any fabric can damage the environment.

Natural

C otton is a natural fibre. But cotton plants are hard on the soil. A lot of pesticides are used on them. Look for unbleached, organically grown cottons.

Wool is also a natural fibre and comes from animals like sheep. Unfortunately, they have to be dipped in a poisonous insecticide to keep bugs off them.

Make a Green Fashion Statement!

PATCH IT!

Start a trend in your school by patching your clothes. You can get or make patches that make "green" statements, like "Patches – A pollution solution!"

WEAR IT!

Wear clothing with messages about the environment.

THINK GREEN

THINK GREEN

THE GREEN SHOPPER

DONATE CLOTHES TO CHARITIES AND SECOND-HAND STORES

- Make sure they are clean and in good condition.
- Pin together matching pieces (such as belts and skirts).
- Drop off clothes on weekdays. (On weekends the boxes overflow.)
- Give the school dance a theme like the "fifties" or "sixties". You won't need to but new clothes – you can wear ones from the attic or second-hand ones.
- Organize a school or neighbourhood "clothes swap day."

Buy Second-Hand

Synthetic

Synthetic fibres include polyester, nylon, acrylic, and rayon. All but rayon are made from petroleum – a non-renewable resource. Rayon is made from wood. Making synthetic fibres causes pollution too.

GREEN JEWELLERY

♦ Jewellery can be fun to wear. But it makes sense to buy pieces that will last instead of a lot of cheap stuff that you end up throwing away.

♦ Fashion watches look sharp, but some last only as long as the battery. So look for ones that have replaceable batteries and excellent guarantees. Better yet, buy one that doesn't need a battery (solar or wind-up).

♦ You also need to think about where jewellery comes from. Remember, for instance, that elephants are killed to get ivory and reefs are destroyed to get coral.

♦ Mining gold and diamonds causes pollution too.

DON'T BUY THROWAWAY WATCHES

Nature the Natural Way

Whenever you are out in a natural area, think of yourself as a guest in someone else's home. All plants and animals – even the tiniest – have their place in the natural world. They all work together to create a delicate balance, and you have to be very careful not to disturb that natural harmony.

Next time you have a chance to camp, hike, canoe, backback, stay at a cottage, or visit a conservation area or local park, pretend you're a fugitive! Don't leave any trace that you were ever there!

Here are some guidelines to help you:

● Don't take *anything* from the wilderness – you don't know whose ecosystem you might be upsetting.

● Do not leave any garbage behind – it can kill animals who eat it.

● Don't strip bark from any tree or carve anything into the trunk. It can badly harm living trees, and ones that look dead might not really be.

● Camp only on established campsites.

● If you have to put a tent on grass or plants, move the tent every day or two.

● Don't cut live branches to make shelters or mattresses.

● Never cut live trees for tent poles.

● Use a dishpan to wash everything – including yourself! Dump the dirty water at least 40 m away from lakes and streams.

● Use only biodegradable soaps and shampoos.

● Use a campstove, not a campfire.

● If you have to make a fire, use only old, dry wood. Use existing firepits.

Clean up after others if they weren't as careful as they should have been!

- Use existing outhouses and latrines whenever you can.

- If you have to make a latrine, dig it at least 40 m away from any water. You need to dig the hole only about 15 to 20 cm deep. Use recycled, unbleached toilet paper. Bury everything completely.

GOING FISHING?

- **Don't use lead sinkers! Waterbirds eat them and die a slow, painful death from lead poisoning.**

- **Be very careful with your fishing line. Lost or thrown-away line can strangle animals.**

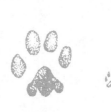

CARDINAL CAMPING R·U·L·E

CARRY OUT EVERY-THING YOU CARRIED IN. BASH IT, BAG IT, BRING IT BACK OUT.

CAT

RACCOON

DOG

RABBIT

THE GREEN DETECTIVE

TRACKS TELL A STORY!

Learning to track is a lot like learning to read. An animal writes the story of its daily life with footprints and other marks it leaves behind. The environment becomes an exciting book – and the tracker knows how to read it.

Tracking is a real art but it's not hard to learn. A parent or teacher can get the book *Tom Brown's Field Guide to Nature and Survival for Children* and help you learn from it.

To be a real tracker, you have to learn to be quiet and patient, and you must keep your eyes and ears open – just like the best detectives. Here are some animal signs to look for besides tracks:

➤ Scratches on trees
➤ Chewed or gnawed plants
➤ Signs of digging
➤ Trails or broken vegetation
➤ Fur or feathers
➤ Tramped-down sleeping areas

Celebrate!
And Be Good to the Earth

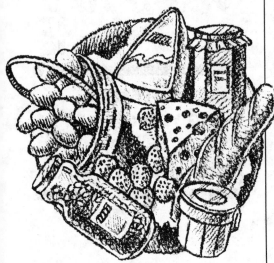

We buy so much during the holidays and for special occasions. So to be a Green Shopper, you have to limit the amount you buy – and learn to buy environment-friendly things. You must also limit what you ask others to buy for you.

We also use a lot of wrapping paper and disposable items during holidays and on birthdays. Here are some ways you can make these celebrations greener!

Give Greener Gifts

Make gifts for others whenever you can. Homemade jams and jellies and baked goods packed in reusable tins are always appreciated! If you buy presents, choose ones that are environment-friendly, for example:

- Cruelty-free, biodegradable body-care products.
- Packages of wildflower seeds to plant.
- Environmental books or magazine subscriptions. (See the list at the back of this book.)
- Bird feeders.
- A blank-page book to use as a diary of nature observations.
- Books and science kits that help people learn about nature.
- Binoculars and a bird guide.
- Acid rain test kit.

THE GREEN SHOPPER
SAVE THE TREES THAT ARE CUT DOWN TO MAKE WRAPPING PAPER!

- Use reusable cloth bags, ribbons, and bows instead of paper wrap and decorations.
- Reuse paper wrap, ribbons, and bows.
- Make your own wrapping paper out of newspaper, coloured comics, paper bags, wallpaper scraps, or glossy magazine pages.
- Create your own wrapping paper designs. Decorate with drawings, paintings, or make prints. Library books can give you more ideas.
- Make the wrapping a part of the present. Scarves, tea towels, T-shirts, bandanas, and pillowcases all work well.

Have an Earth-Friendly Holiday...

And leave a little bit of our country more beautiful than it was!

Combine an environment-friendly picnic with a beach or natural area cleanup.

● Pick an area the whole family can bicycle to or take public transportation to.

● After cleaning up the litter others have left, celebrate with a litterless lunch.

● Serve healthy, organically grown, home-cooked food instead of overpackaged convenience foods.

● Pack it all in reusable containers.

● Take drinks in refillable containers.

● Use real dishes and cutlery instead of paper or plastic ones.

You'll have a great time – and no one will have to remind you to clean up after yourselves!

SAVE THOSE GREETING CARDS!

■ Glue blank paper over the old message inside and write a new one.

■ Cut up old cards to make new ones or gift tags.

■ If you do buy cards, purchase ones on recycled paper from an environmental group – and support their cause.

HOLD ON TO THOSE BALLOONS!

Balloons are fun to have at parties. But, believe it or not, a balloon can float through the air for thousands of kilometres and make its way to the ocean.

Balloons in the water look like jellyfish. Sea turtles, whales, and other sea animals eat them. The balloons get stuck in their throats and stomachs, and the animals die.

If your balloon bursts, put the plastic bits in the garbage.

Hang on to your balloons – especially ones filled with helium. Help younger kids keep their balloons by tying the strings carefully around their wrists.

Celebrations that release thousands of balloons into the sky are very harmful. If you hear of one, tell the organizers about the problems!

Suggest an alternative, such as a kite-flying day.

Instead of giving a gift, do something for someone! Make them breakfast in bed, offer to do their chores for a week, take them on a nature walk, or get the whole family to do a volunteer service together.

Home and School Audits

If you'd like to find out how environmentally responsible your home and school are, you can do an audit. Conducting an audit is a little like giving a test because you can ask a lot of questions. You will need to consider what is bought, what is used, and what is wasted. The home audit is a good project to do with the whole family. The school audit is fun to do with your class, because you finally get a chance to test the school!

These checklists include some of the things you'll want to consider. The more times you can answer YES, the better.

Use your imagination and borrow ideas from other helpful books (see the list at the back of this book) to come up with many other ways to make your home and school even greener!

How Green Is Your Home?

This book has shown you that there are many ways to make your lifestyle friendlier to the environment. You've already learned how important it is to purchase only what you really need and to reuse or recycle everything you can. Now it's time to get your family together and take a tour of your home.

Keep a diary of the things you do to make your home a little greener. You can find out how much water and energy you use by reading the meter or checking the utility bills your family receives. And you can weigh how much paper and other garbage you throw away each week. Including charts and graphs in your diary will show you how well you are doing. You can challenge your relatives and your neighbours to see who can have the "Greenest Home on the Block."

The 3 Rs – reduce, reuse, recycle – are the basis of environment-friendly living.

Saving water and energy is important. Has your family bought or installed:

YES NO
- ☐ ☐ a low-flow shower head?
- ☐ ☐ a jug or dam in the toilet water tank?
- ☐ ☐ low-energy compact fluorescent lighting?
- ☐ ☐ dimmer switches on your lights?
- ☐ ☐ a ceiling fan (instead of an air conditioner)?
- ☐ ☐ a heat pump?
- ☐ ☐ a battery recharger?
- ☐ ☐ double- or triple-glazed windows?

- ☐ ☐ Do you take short showers rather than full baths?
- ☐ ☐ Do you turn the water off while brushing your teeth and shampooing your hair?

YES NO
- ☐ ☐ Do you turn off the lights, the television, and the stereo when you leave the room?
- ☐ ☐ Do you keep a jug of cold water in the fridge (instead of letting the tap run every time you want a cold drink)?
- ☐ ☐ Are all appliances regularly cleaned and kept in good working order?

Are the following areas well insulated:

YES NO
- ☐ ☐ the roof and attic?
- ☐ ☐ the water tank and pipes?
- ☐ ☐ around the doors (with draft-proof stripping)?
- ☐ ☐ around the windows?

☞ Continued on page 96

Who will have the Greenest Home on the Block?

YES NO
- ☑ ☐ Do you use a clothesline on sunny days to dry your clothes?
- ☐ ☐ Do you keep your thermostat at 20°C or lower in the winter?
- ☐ ☐ Have you planted trees to shelter the house from cold winter winds and the hot summer sun?

Do you collect and recycle:

YES NO
- ☐ ☐ newspapers?
- ☐ ☐ aluminum and tin cans?
- ☐ ☐ glass bottles and jars?
- ☐ ☐ plastic?
- ☐ ☐ used clothes?

YES NO
- ☐ ☐ Do you compost your kitchen and yard waste?
- ☐ ☐ Do you keep a chalkboard or scrap paper next to the telephone for messages?
- ☐ ☐ Do you save scrap paper so you can draw or paint on the other side?
- ☐ ☐ Do you keep your household hazardous wastes (old paints, batteries, used motor oil, etc.) for collection on special waste days or take them to special depots?

Buying environment-friendly groceries and household supplies is one of the most important things your family can do.

YES NO
- ☐ ☐ Do you save reusable containers to store bulk foods?
- ☐ ☐ Does your family eat organically grown foods?
- ☐ ☐ Do you buy local, in-season produce?
- ☐ ☐ Do you eat at least one meatless main meal every week?

Do you avoid buying the following disposable products:

YES NO
- ☐ ☐ disposable diapers?
- ☐ ☐ throwaway razors?
- ☐ ☐ paper towels and napkins?
- ☐ ☐ paper plates and cups?
- ☐ ☐ disposable lighters?
- ☐ ☐ disposable pens?
- ☐ ☐ disposable cameras?

YES NO
- ☐ ☐ Do you use a basket or cloth shopping bag?
- ☐ ☐ Do you buy recycled paper products (such as toilet paper)?
- ☐ ☐ Have you replaced toxic cleaners with environmentally safe alternatives such as pure soap flakes, baking soda, and vinegar?
- ☐ ☐ Do you use biodegradable, phosphate-free washing products?
- ☐ ☐ Do you use cosmetics and body-care products (like soaps and shampoos) that are biodegradable and cruelty-free?

☞ Continued on page 97

YES NO
- ☐ ☐ Are all your soft drinks bought in returnable containers?
- ☐ ☐ Is your home a No Smoking home?

If you have a short trip to make, do you use:

YES NO
- ☐ ☐ your feet?
- ☐ ☐ your bicycle?
- ☐ ☐ public transportation?

The School Audit

Get together with your teacher and class to plan your audit. Assign each person in your class a specific job to do or area to look at. You might want to gather information and opinions using questionnaires, interviews, and active investigation.

When you have completed the audit, you can write up an official report of your findings. Make suggestions about changes that could be made. Draw some graphs so that you can chart the progress and results of any changes you suggest.

It is important to realize that schools have to follow certain rules. This may mean that some of the suggestions you make will require that the rules be changed. For example, health departments say that very strong cleaners must be used in schools. Maybe there are safer – and more environment-friendly – alternatives. Discuss your suggestions with the health department, your principal, the caretakers, and the school board.

In the Classroom

Do students use:

YES NO
- ☐ ☐ refillable pens and pencils?
- ☐ ☐ non-toxic art materials?
- ☐ ☐ recycled notepaper and computer paper?
- ☐ ☐ solar-powered calculators?

- ☐ ☐ In your classroom do you discuss environmental issues?

YES NO
- ☐ ☐ Do you take fieldtrips to help you learn about the environment?
- ☐ ☐ Do you try to come up with solutions to environmental problems?
- ☐ ☐ Does your school or class have a group membership to an environmental group?

☞ Continued on page 98

CHECKING YOUR art MATERIALS

THINGS TO AVOID	THINGS TO USE INSTEAD
Turpentine, toluene, rubber-cement thinner	Water-based products only
Epoxy, instant glue, model glue	White glue or school paste
Permanent felt markers	Water-colour markers
Powdered clay	Talc-free or pre-mixed clay (Wash tables after using.)
Powdered tempera paints	Liquid paints (The teacher can pre-mix powders.)
Pastels, chalk, or dry markers that create dust	Crayons, oil pastels, and dustless chalks

NEVER USE ANY PAINT, INK, OR GLAZE THAT CONTAINS LEAD

Close Drapes on Sunny Summer Days

Open Drapes on Sunny Winter Days

In the Building

Are the following areas well insulated:

YES NO

☐ ☐ the roof?
☐ ☐ the water tank and pipes?
☐ ☐ around the outside doors?
☐ ☐ around the windows?

Do students, teachers, and caretakers:

YES NO

☐ ☐ turn off lights when they're not needed?
☐ ☐ close blinds or drapes on sunny summer days to keep rooms cool?
☐ ☐ open drapes or blinds on sunny winter days to heat rooms naturally?
☐ ☐ close off rooms that are not being used so that they don't need to be heated or cooled?

Does your school have the following energy-efficient equipment:

YES NO

☐ ☐ energy-efficient lighting?
☐ ☐ energy-efficient windows?
☐ ☐ a programmable thermostat?
☐ ☐ fans (instead of an air conditioner)?
☐ ☐ window-warming kits?

Do the caretakers:

YES NO

☐ ☐ check your school regularly for drafts and leaks?
☐ ☐ make repairs if necessary?

☐ ☐ Does your school use biodegradable and cruelty-free cleaners?

YES NO

☐ ☐ Does your school donate used things such as books, clothes, gym equipment, and furniture to places like libraries, daycare centres, and neighbourhood groups?

Does your school recycle:

YES NO

☐ ☐ fine paper?
☐ ☐ newspaper?

In the washrooms does your school use:

YES NO

☐ ☐ recycled toilet paper?
☐ ☐ recycled paper towels?
☐ ☐ biodegradable, cruelty-free hand soap?

Does your school library have:

YES NO

☐ ☐ an environmental resource centre?
☐ ☐ books on environmental issues?
☐ ☐ subscriptions to environmental magazines?
☐ ☐ a bulletin board for recent environmental stories and newspaper clippings?

Does the school office use:

YES NO

☐ ☐ recycled notepaper?
☐ ☐ recycled computer paper?
☐ ☐ recycled photocopy paper?
☐ ☐ both sides of the paper when photocopying?
☐ ☐ solar-powered calculators and adding machines?

☞ Continued on page 99

Does your school have:

YES NO
- ☐ ☐ a conservation club?
- ☐ ☐ a recycling club?
- ☐ ☐ an environmental club?

- ☐ ☐ Does your class or school raise money to donate to environmental groups?

Does your class or school organize or participate in:

YES NO
- ☐ ☐ environmental fairs?
- ☐ ☐ schoolyard and neighbourhood clean-up campaigns?
- ☐ ☐ recycling projects?
- ☐ ☐ bike-to-school weeks?

In the Cafeteria or Lunchroom

Does this room use:

YES NO
- ☐ ☐ refillable containers for things like salt and ketchup?
- ☐ ☐ reusable cutlery and dishes?
- ☐ ☐ unpackaged or minimally packaged products?
- ☐ ☐ reusable meal trays?
- ☐ ☐ refillable or recyclable drink containers?

Are these disposables avoided:

YES NO
- ☐ ☐ plastic or paper bags?
- ☐ ☐ paper napkins?
- ☐ ☐ plastic straws wrapped in paper?

- ☐ ☐ Do most students and staff who bring their lunches bring litterless lunches?
- ☐ ☐ Are there bins for recycling cans and glass bottles?

Around the Grounds

YES NO
- ☐ ☐ Have trees been planted around your school to keep the building shaded in summer and insulated in winter?

Does your school use any of these natural methods of pest control instead of using harmful pesticides:

YES NO
- ☐ ☐ feeders and houses to attract insect-eating birds?
- ☐ ☐ organic pesticides?
- ☐ ☐ pay students to pull up weeds?

- ☐ ☐ Is there a garden where fruits or vegetables are grown organically?

YES NO
- ☐ ☐ Is there a compost pile where you can dispose of leftover food and schoolyard waste?

Do students and staff use these energy-efficient transportation methods to get to school:

YES NO
- ☐ ☐ walking?
- ☐ ☐ bicycling?
- ☐ ☐ public transportation?
- ☐ ☐ car pooling?

- ☐ ☐ Does your school encourage people to ride their bikes by providing plenty of bike racks?

Many schools built in the 1970s have asbestos in them. Does yours?
* Find out what asbestos is, where it is used, and why it is harmful.
* Some schools with asbestos have already taken care of the problem. *Has yours?*

Some Schools Have Lead Water Pipes or Lead Soldering.

Lead can get into the water when it sits overnight in the pipes. Lead is very harmful.

● Does your school have this problem?

● Can the lead pipes be changed?

● If not, water should be run on every floor for five minutes first thing in the morning before anyone drinks it. It should then be fine for the rest of the day.

The Green Team
Keeps up the good work

You can do hundreds of fun and interesting things to save the environment. You help make a difference every time you learn more about nature and the ecosystem, take action in an environmental cause, or use your buying power to tell companies you want "green" products. Here are some more activities and important ideas for you to think about.

WARNING: POLLUTION AHEAD!

You probably spend a lot of time outdoors, playing in fields, exploring woods, and just hanging out with friends in vacant lots.

These are just the sorts of places where illegal dumpers try to get rid of toxic wastes and dangerous chemicals. Drums full of poisons may even have been dumped there before you were born. These things can be deadly!

Watch for the signs of pollution listed below whenever you are playing outdoors. If you see them, report them immediately to a parent, teacher, or the Ministry or Department of the Environment. **Do not touch anything! Don't even get close!** You must leave that to people who have the proper safety equipment.

- Strangely coloured soil or signs of spilled oil
- Unusual smells
- Piles of waste or garbage
- Abandoned, rusty drums
- Dead or sick wildlife
- Dead or dying plants
- Open-ended pipes
- Strange colours or oily films in ponds or streams
- Stains or filth left by trickling water or on the bottom of streams

Stay away from these things and you'll keep yourself safe! Report them and you'll help keep others safe. You'll also be doing planet Earth a big favour!

THE GREEN
Scientist

GROW A DIRTLESS GARDEN

Grow a garden in water instead of dirt! It's called hydroponic gardening. This is an especially good method for growing vegetables because it is done without pesticides and it doesn't cause soil erosion.
(Based on an activity in Foodworks.)

What You Need:

👁 a wide-mouth jar for each plant

👁 a flower pot that fits just inside the mouth of the jar

👁 thick cotton rope

👁 seeds (radishes, lettuce, and green beans work well)

👁 vermiculite and hydroponic fertilizer from a garden centre

What You Do:

👁 Cut your rope so it reaches from the bottom of the jar to about two-thirds of the way up the flower pot.

👁 Fray both ends of the rope to make a wick that will suck up water.

👁 Poke the rope through the hole in the bottom of the pot.

👁 Hold it in position and pack vermiculite around it.

👁 Mix the hydroponic fertilizer with water. (Follow the directions on the package.)

👁 Pour some water/fertilizer mixture in the jar – but make sure the water doesn't touch the bottom of the flower pot once the pot is in position.

👁 Put the pot in the jar so the wick hangs in the water.

👁 Plant two or three seeds in the vermiculite.

Hydroponic gardening works because plants don't really need dirt to grow. They need dirt only to hold them up. They get their food from the nutrients in the soil that come from decaying plants and animals. What's supporting the plants in your hydroponic garden? Where are they getting their food? Do you think you could grow plants without water?

THE GREEN SHOPPER

PLANT A TREE IN AFRICA

Buy someone a gift that might last for a hundred years! Plant a tree in Africa in their name. Trees in many African countries have been damaged by drought, destroyed by overgrazing by animals, and cut for fuel. Without trees the soil erodes, and not enough food can be grown. In Ethiopia, for example, 90% of the trees have been destroyed.

To plant trees as a gift, write to:
Canadian Physicians for Aid and Relief
64 Charles Street East
Toronto, Ontario
M4Y 1T1

You can plant 60 trees for only $15!

CPAR will send you a beautiful full-colour poster inscribed with the name of the person you made the donation for.

THE GREEN DETECTIVE

ON THE TRACKING TRAIL

Make plaster casts of animal tracks! Then you can take the casts home to study them and make a collection of all the tracks you find. You can even take all the ingredients you'll need in a backpack when you go for a hike.

What You Need:

➤➤ strips of light-weight cardboard about 8 cm high and 30 cm long

➤➤ several big paper clips

➤➤ a small bag of plaster of Paris from a craft or hardware store

➤➤ a container of water with a tight-fitting lid

➤➤ a spoon

What You Do:

➤➤ Read the directions on the plaster of Paris so you'll have a good idea how much plaster and water you'll need to take with you.

➤➤ Look for a good, clear animal footprint.

➤➤ Very carefully remove any pebbles, sticks, or leaves that are in or around it.

➤➤ Use the paper clips to fasten a strip of cardboard into a ring that fits around the track.

➤➤ Push the ring gently but firmly into the dirt around the track.

➤➤ Sprinkle plaster of Paris into the water until the surface of the water is covered.

➤➤ Stir the mixture until the plaster is all absorbed.

➤➤ Keep adding plaster and stirring until your mixture is about as thick as soft ice cream.

➤➤ Carefully pour the mixture into the cardboard ring so that it's about 4 cm deep.

➤➤ Wait 20 to 30 minutes until the plaster is hard.

➤➤ Gently pick up the cast and blow off any dirt.

➤➤ Take the track home and find out what made it – if you don't already know.

Write Letters to Get Action!

Since you can't always talk to important people in person or on the phone, writing letters is a good way to let them know what environmental issues are important to you.

Here are some tips to help you write a good letter.

- *Be polite. You want the person to listen to your view.*
- *Be personal. Use your own words.*
- *Recommend action. Say what you would like the person to do about your concerns. Ask for something specific, such as support for a ban on whale hunting or a law against balloon launches.*
- *Ask for a reply. This will force the person to think seriously about your concerns.*
- *Send copies to other concerned people. If the person knows that other people have seen your letter, he or she may be more likely to respond. Let the person know who else has received a copy of your letter by typing "c.c.:" at the bottom with a list of the people's names.*
- *Check the information. Make sure the person's name, title, and address are complete and correct. A teacher or other adult can help you. You can find many addresses in the Blue Pages of your telephone book. Some are listed in the back of this book.*
- *Encourage other people to write letters too. The more people that write, the greater the influence you'll have. Maybe you can organize a letter-writing campaign at your school!*

Who to write to:

- *For national issues, write to your member of Parliament. Send copies (c.c.) to the prime minister and the appropriate cabinet minister. (If you don't know the name of your member of Parliament, call 1-800-267-8683 to find out.)*
- *For provincial issues, write to your member of provincial Parliament or Legislature. Send copies to the premier and appropriate cabinet minister.*
- *If you have concerns about products, write to the company's president.*

Thinking Green— Means Thinking!

People who "Think Green" all the time are called environmentalists. This book is full of facts and ideas that most environmentalists believe are very important. But you will soon discover that not everyone agrees with what environmentalists believe.

It is important for you to realize that environmental issues and solutions are not simple. There are many sides to every question, and different people have different values. Our values affect the decisions we make. Fixing environmental problems might cause other problems or disrupt some people's lives.

For example, think about how recycling paper might affect people and the economy.

● If everyone begins to recycle paper, we are going to cut down far fewer trees.

● Hooray! That's just what everyone wants, right?

● But what about people who work as lumberjacks? Or in sawmills? Or in pulp and paper plants? How will they feel? What might happen to their jobs?

● Can you think of any other problems recycling paper might cause?

● More important, can you think of solutions? For instance, can you think of changes these industries might begin to make now so they could protect their employees and be ready for the future?

● What do you think the consequences would be if everyone decided *not* to recycle paper?

Good environmentalists know there are many sides to every question.

They also know there is only one set of facts. They learn all the facts – and weigh them carefully before they take a stand on any issue.

GETTING THE FACTS – DRAWING CONCLUSIONS

This is a good project for your class.

■ Select a number of industries that might affect the environment in your province. Mining, trapping, fishing, farming with pesticides, and making plastics are just a few.

■ Work in groups to gather all the facts you can. Find out the different sides of the question.

■ Consider the effect the industry is having on the environment.

■ Consider the benefits that come from the industry.

■ Consider the effects of solving the environmental problem.

■ Weigh all the facts – and come up with creative solutions that will solve all the problems!

■ People may listen to your solutions now, or someday you may have a job where you can put some of them into practice!

Groups for More Information

Canadian Coalition on Acid Rain
112 St. Clair Avenue West
Suite 401, Toronto
ON M4V 2Y3 (416) 968-2135

Canadian Federation of Humane Societies
30 Concourse Gate, Suite 102
Nepean, ON K2E 7V7
(613) 224-8072

Canadian Nature Federation
453 Sussex Drive
Ottawa, ON K1N 6Z4
(613) 238-6154
(inquire about provincial and local naturalist groups)

Canadian Organic Growers
Box 6408, Station J
Ottawa, ON K2A 3Y6
(613) 259-2967

Canadian Parks and Wilderness Society
160 Bloor Street East, Suite 1150
Toronto, ON M4W 1B9
(416) 972-0868
(inquire about provincial and local naturalist groups)

Canadian Wildlife Federation
1673 Carling Avenue
Ottawa, ON K2A 1C4
(613) 725-2191

Canadian Wildlife Service
25 St. Clair Avenue East
Toronto, ON M4T 1M2
(416) 965-4251

The Children's Rainforest
PO Box 936, Leniston
ME 04240 USA
JUST FOR KIDS

Energy Probe
225 Brunswick Avenue
Toronto, ON M5S 2M6
(416) 978-7014

Environmental Youth Alliance
PO Box 29031
1996 West Broadway
Vancouver, BC V6J 5C2
(604) 737-2258
JUST FOR KIDS

Environmentally Sound Packaging Coalition
2150 Maple Street
Vancouver, BC V6J 3T3
(604) 736-3644

Friends of the Earth
251 Laurier Avenue West
Suite 701, Ottawa
ON K1P 5J6 (613) 230-3352

Greenpeace
578 Bloor Street West
Toronto, ON M6G 1K1
(416) 538-6470

The HOOT Club
c/o *OWL* Magazine
Suite 304
56 The Esplanade
Toronto, ON M5E 1A7
JUST FOR KIDS

Pollution Probe
12 Madison Avenue
Toronto, ON M5R 2S1
(416) 926-1907

Probe International
225 Brunswick Avenue
Toronto, ON M5S 2M6
(416) 978-7014

Sierra Club of Eastern Canada
2316 Queen Street East
Toronto, ON M4E 1G8
(416) 698-8446

Sierra Club of Western Canada
620 View Street, #314
Victoria, BC V8W 3T8
(604) 386-5255

Société pour vaincre la pollution
CP 65, Succursale Place d'Armes
Montreal, PQ H2Y 3E9
(514) 844-5477

Solar Energy Society
15 York Street, Suite 3
Ottawa, ON K1N 5S7
(613) 236-4594

Temagami Wilderness Society
19 Mercer Street, Suite 307
Toronto, ON M5V 1H2
(416) 599-0152

Western Canada Wilderness Committee
20 Water Street
Vancouver, BC V6B 1A4
(604) 683-8220

World Wildlife Fund (Canada)
60 St. Clair Avenue East
Suite 201, Toronto
ON M4T 1N5
(416) 923-8173

World Society for the Protection of Animals
215 Lakeshore Boulevard East
Suite 211, Toronto
ON M5A 3W9
(416) 369-0044

Environmental Networks

Canadian Environmental Network
PO Box 1289, Station B
Ottawa, ON K1P 5R3
(613) 563-2078
(inquire about provincial networks)

Atlantic Environmental Network
3115 Veith Street, 3rd Floor
Halifax, NS B3K 3G9
(902) 454-2139

Réseau québécois des groupes écologistes
CP 1480
Succursale Place d'Armes
Montreal, PQ H2Y 3K8
(514) 982-9444

Ontario Environment Network
Box 125, Station P, Toronto
ON M5T 2Z7 (416) 925-1322

Manitoba Eco-Network
PO Box 3125, Winnipeg
MB R3C 4E6 (204) 956-1468

Saskatchewan Eco-Network
PO Box 1372, Saskatoon
SK S7K 0G4 (306) 665-1915

Alberta Environmental Network
10511 Saskatchewan Drive
Edmonton, AB T6E 4S1
(403) 465-0872

British Columbia Environmental Network
2150 Maple Street
Vancouver, BC V6J 3T3
(604) 733-2400

Northern Environmental Network
PO Box 4163, Whitehorse
YT Y1A 3S9 (403) 668-5687

Recycling Organizations

Ecology Action Centre
3115 Veith Street, 3rd Floor
Halifax, NS B3K 3G9
(902) 454-7828

Fonds québécois de récuperation
407 Saint Laurent Boulevard,
Suite 500, Montreal
PQ H2Y 2Y5 (514) 874-3701

Recycling Council of Ontario
489 College Street, Room 504
Toronto, ON M6G 1A5
1-800-263-2849

Recycling Council of Manitoba
412 McDermot Avenue
Winnipeg, MB R3A 0A9
(204) 942-7781

Recycling Council of British Columbia
2150 Maple Street, Vancouver
BC V6J 3T3 (604) 731-7222

Federal Government

Department of External Affairs & International Trade
Lester B. Pearson Bldg.
125 Sussex Drive,
Ottawa, ON K1A 0G2
(613) 996-9134

Department of Energy, Mines and Resources
580 Booth Street, Ottawa
ON K1A 0E4 (613) 995-3065

Department of Forestry
Ottawa, ON K1A 1G5
(819) 997-1107

Department of the Environment
Ottawa, ON K1A 0H3
(819) 997-2800

REGIONAL OFFICES

Environment Canada Atlantic Region
15th Floor, 45 Alderney Drive
Dartmouth, NS B2Y 2N6
(902) 426-7990

Environment Canada Quebec Region
CP 6060, 3 Buade Street
4th Floor, Quebec
PQ G1R 4V7 (418) 648-7204

Environment Canada Ontario Region
25 St. Clair Avenue East
6th Floor, Toronto
ON M4T 1M2 (416) 973-6467

Environment Canada Western and Northern Region
2nd Floor, 4999-98 Avenue
Edmonton, AB T6B 2X3
(403) 468-8075

Environment Canada Pacific and Yukon Region
Communications Directorate
3rd Floor, Kapilano 100
Park Royal South
West Vancouver, BC V7T 1A2
(604) 666-5900

Provincial and Territorial Governments

NEWFOUNDLAND

Department of Environment and Lands
PO Box 8700, St. John's
NF A1B 4J6 (709) 576-3394

Department of Forestry
PO Box 8700, St. John's
NF A1B 4J6 (709) 576-3245

NOVA SCOTIA

Department of the Environment
PO Box 2107, Halifax
NS B3J 3B7 (902) 424-5300

Department of Lands and Forests
PO Box 698, Halifax
NS B3J 2T9 (902) 424-5935

NEW BRUNSWICK

Department of the Environment
PO Box 6000, Fredericton
NB E3B 5H1 (506) 453-3700

Department of Natural Resources and Energy
PO Box 6000, Fredericton
NB E3B 5H1 (506) 453-2614

PRINCE EDWARD ISLAND

Department of the Environment
PO Box 2000, Charlottetown
PE C1A 7N8 (902) 368-5280

Department of Energy and Forestry
PO Box 2000, Charlottetown
PE C1A 7N8 (902) 368-5010

QUEBEC

Ministère de l'Environnement
3900, rue Marly, Ste-Foy
PQ G1X 4E4 (418) 643-6071

Ministère de l'énergie et des ressources
200, ch. Ste-Foy, 7 étage
Quebec, PQ G1R 4X7
(418) 643-8060

ONTARIO

Ministry of the Environment
135 St. Clair Avenue West
Toronto, ON M4V 1P5
(416) 323-4321

Ministry of Natural Resources
Whitney Block
99 Wellesley Street West
Toronto, ON M7A 1W3
(416) 965-2000

MANITOBA

Department of Environment
330 St. Mary Avenue
Winnipeg, MB R3C 3Z5
(204) 945-4742

Department of Natural Resources
1495 St. James Street
Winnipeg, MB R3H 0W9
(204) 945-6658

SASKATCHEWAN

Department of the Environment and Public Safety
3085 Albert Street, Regina
SK S4S 0B1 (306) 787-6113

Saskatchewan Parks and Renewable Resources
3211 Albert Street, Regina
SK S4S 5W6 (306) 787-2700

ALBERTA

Department of the Environment
Oxbridge Place
9820-106 Street, Edmonton
AB T5K 2J6 (403) 427-2739

Department of Forestry, Lands and Wildlife
9915-108 Street, Edmonton
AB T5K 2C9 (403) 427-3590

BRITISH COLUMBIA

Ministry of Environment
Parliament Buildings, Victoria
BC V8V 1X5 (604) 387-1161

Ministry of Parks
4000 Seymour Place, 3rd Floor
Victoria, BC V8V 1X5
(604) 356-7043

Ministry of Forests
1450 Government Street
Victoria, BC V8W 3E7
(604) 387-5255

NORTHWEST TERRITORIES

Department of Renewable Resources
PO Box 1320, Yellowknife
NT X1A 2L9 (403) 873-7420

YUKON TERRITORY

Department of Renewable Resources
PO Box 2703, Whitehorse,
YT Y1A 2C6 (403) 667-5634

Free Things to Send Away For

Call, write, or visit the department or ministry in charge of environmental issues in your province (see page 108). Also contact recycling organizations (see page 107) and local groups. Ask them to send you a list of their publications along with any free material available for kids. Here are just a few of the things you can get – free for the asking!

From the federal Department of the Environment
The Green Scene
The Water Primer
What We Can Do for Our
   Environment

From The Canadian Coalition on Acid Rain
The Effects of Acid Rain on the Young
   of Many Species

From the federal Department of Energy, Mines and Resources
Energy for You and Me Colouring Poster
Conserve Energy Poster
Enermagic Magazine
Renewable Energy Colouring Poster

From The Toronto Humane Society
Cruelty Free Shopper's Guide
general pet care pamphlets

From The Canadian Wildlife Federation
Recycle for the Birds
You Can Do It!

From The Canadian Wildlife Service
Wetlands
Bird Feeders and Nest Boxes for Birds
Endangered Species in Canada
Benefits of Wildlife

Books and Magazines

BOOKS FOR KIDS

50 Simple Things Kids Can Do to Save the Earth.
Kansas City, Mo.: The Earthworks Group, 1990.

Beastly Neighbors.
Mollie Rights. Toronto: Little, Brown, 1981.

The Bird Book and The Bird Feeder.
Neil and Karen Dawe. Toronto: Somerville House, 1988.

The Bug Book and The Bug Bottle.
Dr. Hugh Danks. Toronto: Somerville House, 1987.

City Safaris: A Sierra Club Explorer's Guide to Urban Adventures for Grownups and Kids.
Carolyn Shaffer and Erica Fielder. San Francisco: Sierra Club Books, 1987.

Discovering Nature: Things to Do Inside and Outside with Plants and Animals.
Midas Dekkers. Toronto: Stoddart, 1987.

Exploring Your Neighbourhood.
Tom Scanlan. Toronto: Is Five Press, 1984.

Foodworks: An Ontario Science Centre Book of Experiments.
The Centennial Centre of Science and Technology. Toronto: Kids Can Press, 1986.

The Garden Book and The Green House.
Wes Porter. Toronto: Somerville House, 1989.

Good Planets Are Hard to Find!: Ecology Action Workbook and Dictionary.
Ronald Bazar and Roma Dehr. Vancouver: Earth Beat Press, 1990.

Have Fun with Magnifying.
The Centennial Centre of Science and Technology. Toronto: Kids Can Press, 1987.

The Kids' Nature Book: 365 Indoor/ Outdoor Activities and Experiences.
Susan Milord. Charlotte, Vt.: Williamson Publishing, 1989.

Looking at the Environment.
David Suzuki. Toronto: Stoddart, 1989.

The Pond Book and Pail.
Karen and Neil Dawe. Toronto: Somerville House, 1990.

The Puzzlers Book.
Edited by Elizabeth MacLeod. Toronto: Greey de Pencier Books, 1990.

Science Fun with Mud and Dirt.
Rose Wyler. New York: Simon & Schuster, 1986.

Scienceworks: An Ontario Science Centre Book of Experiments.
The Centennial Centre of Science and Technology. Toronto: Kids Can Press, 1984.

Simple Salad Kit: The "Wee" Sprouts.
Rexdale, Ont.: Wee Share Canada, 1988.

Spring Clean Your Planet: Learn All About Pollution from These Easy Exciting Experiments.
Ralph Levinson. London, Eng.: Beaver Books, 1987.

The Super Heroes Super Healthy Cookbook.
Mark Saltzman, Judy Garlan, and Michele Grodner. New York: D.C. Comics, 1981.

Urban Ecology.
Jennifer Cochrane. Hove, East Sussex: Wayland Publishers, 1987.

The Wild Inside: Sierra Club's Guide to the Great Indoors.
Linda Allison. Toronto: Little, Brown, 1988.

The Young Person's Guide to Saving the Planet.
Debbie Silver and Bernadette Vallely. London, Eng.: Virago Press, 1990.

OTHER BOOKS

2 Minutes a Day for a Greener Planet.
Marjorie Lamb. Toronto: Harper Collins, 1990.

The Canadian Green Calendar 1991.
Pollution Probe. Toronto: McClelland & Stewart, 1990.

The Canadian Green Consumer Guide.
Pollution Probe. Toronto: McClelland & Stewart, 1989.

The Great Lakes Primer.
Toronto: Pollution Probe, 1986.

Home and Family Guide: Practical Action for the Environment.
Ottawa: The Harmony Foundation of Canada, 1990.

Save Our Planet: 750 Everyday Ways You Can Help Clean Up the Earth.
Diane MacEachern. New York: Dell, 1990.

Tom Brown's Field Guide to Nature and Survival for Children.
Tom Brown, Jr. New York: The Berkley Publishing Group, 1989.

MAGAZINES

National Geographic WORLD.
National Geographic Society
2111 Watline Avenue, Mississauga, ON L4Z 1P3

OWL: The Discovery Magazine for Children.
Suite 304, 56 The Esplanade, Toronto, ON M5E 1A7

P3: The Earth Based Magazine for Kids.
PO Box 52, Montgomery, VT 05470, USA

ScienceWorld.
730 Broadway, New York, NY 10003, USA

Index

Page numbers in **boldface** indicate Green Team activities.

NOTES

NOTES

116

NOTES

NOTES

118

NOTES

A MESSAGE FOR OUR ADULT READERS

Pollution Probe has been fighting to make this country a little greener for more than 20 years. Acid rain, hazardous waste, energy conservation, the quality of drinking water – each year we provide information on these and other vital issues to thousands of Canadians, from school kids working on projects to professional researchers writing reports.

It's a big, demanding job for a non-profit organization. If you and your family and friends wish to get involved in the work of Pollution Probe, please consider making a tax-deductible donation.

Name _____   City _____

Address _____   Province _____

_____   Postal Code _____

My contribution is: $ _____   I am contributing by: Cheque ☐   Credit Card ☐

Card Name & No _____   Expiry date _____

Pollution Probe is a registered national charity (#0384750-53-13)
Donations, comments, and suggestions will be gratefully received at Pollution Probe, 12 Madison Avenue, Toronto, Ontario M5R 2S1 (phone: 416-926-1907; FAX: 416-926-1601)

Design, Photography, and Illustration

The Watt Group, Toronto, Canada

With additional illustrations as follows:

Robert Meecham/Joe Weissmann

Front Cover and Inside Back Cover

Joe Weissmann

Pages 6/7, 8/9, 11, 12, 13, 16, 18, 22, 23, 27, 29, 30,
31, 33, 35, 39, 42, 47, 49, 57, 59, 60, 62/63, 65, 67, 69,
71, 72, 74, 75, 77, 78, 81, 83, 85, 87, 89, 92, 101, 103

Outside Back Cover

John Etheridge

Pages 14, 15, 20, 22, 24, 26, 28, 34, 36, 40, 44, 46, 50, 51,
53, 54, 55, 56, 58, 72, 75, 76, 80, 82, 84, 88, 90, 92, 95, 96, 98

Printed and bound in the United States